Angels:
Our Guardians in Spiritual Battle

ANGELS

Our Guardians in Spiritual Battle

Rev. Msgr. J. Brian Bransfield

Our Sunday Visitor
Huntington, Indiana

Nihil Obstat
Msgr. Michael Heintz, Ph.D.
Censor Librorum

Imprimatur
✠ Kevin C. Rhoades
Bishop of Fort Wayne-South Bend
April 22, 2022

The *Nihil Obstat* and *Imprimatur* are official declarations that a book is free from doctrinal or moral error. It is not implied that those who have granted the *Nihil Obstat* and *Imprimatur* agree with the contents, opinions, or statements expressed.

Our Sunday Visitor Publishing Division
Our Sunday Visitor, Inc.
200 Noll Plaza
Huntington, IN 46750
www.osv.com
1-800-348-2440

ISBN: 978-1-68192-976-7 (Inventory No. T2714)
1. RELIGION—Christian Theology—Angelology & Demonology.
2. RELIGION—Christian Living—Spiritual Growth.
3. RELIGION—Christianity—Catholic.

eISBN: 978-1-68192-977-4
LCCN: 2022937328

Cover and interior design: Chelsea Alt
Cover art: Luca Giordano, "The Prophet Balaam Traveling on his Ass." Restored Traditions

PRINTED IN THE UNITED STATES OF AMERICA

For
Eric Dezenhall

"The angel replied:
'I will go with you;
I am familiar with the way ..."'
(Tobit 5:6, RSV2CE)

CONTENTS

MEETING THE ANGELS

I met my first angel over forty years ago. It was the early 1970s, and I was barely eight years old. Actually, I did not just meet one angel — I met three, and they appeared in an ordinary, yet unexpected way: on television. One night, there was a movie on about the Bible (I cannot remember the title), and as I lay on the sofa in our living room, the screen glowed to life with a scene from the Book of Genesis. It was the story of the great patriarch Abraham. At my young age, I had not yet heard the story of Abraham, so my mom was explaining his story to me. As the scene began, she said, "This is where he meets the angels." As it turns out, in a manner of speaking, so did I.

I expected to see figures with fragile wings and porcelain-like cherub faces reclining on puffy, white clouds. But these angels did not float. Instead of delicate, feathered wings, the angelic figures had an immediate, commanding, and adventurous steadiness about them. Rather than reclining in bleach-white robes, the angels wore long, almost motionless, earth-tone robes, with deep hoods that concealed their faces in quiet shadow. These three sturdy figures stood up straight and tall, conveying confident strength. Their feet were firmly planted on the ground. Their posture was stable, poised, and ready. Their silence was meaningful, their bearing direct. They were dignified, determined, and decisive, and there was a security about them.

But there was more. They stood still, but their presence carried a suggestion of gentle swiftness and unobtrusive purpose. They were accessible, down-to-earth, and within reach — yet at the same time, they were quietly elusive, concealed, and ungraspable. They seemed to stand on the threshold of visibility and invisibility. Yet they were not intimidating. It was as if there were no fear these three angels could not handle. The scene conveyed to me an initial sense of what I would later read from St. Augustine: "There is a certain greatness in the Angels; and such power, that if the Angels exert it to the full, it cannot be withstood."[1] The scene likewise conveyed the sentiments of H. M. Boudon, the seventeenth-century French abbot, spiritual author, and inspiration for St. Louis de Montfort: "There is nothing in created being more powerful than the angelic nature."[2] There was something silently visible, and at the same time, a sense of invisible definition that drew me farther into their mystery. They captured my attention and pulled me along to that mysterious edge between expectation and surprise.

All of this came to me in the space of two or three seconds. Obviously, something more was going on than simply Hollywood's attempt to portray angels. Of course, some people would say all I saw from my vantage point on our living room sofa was well-cast actors in costume. But these figures defied all the stereotypes of angels. Four decades later, the scene remains crisp in my mind's eye, as if I just saw it only a few brief moments ago. After all, angels have a timeless quality about them. And they defy expectations, laying aside stereotypes. Angels appear in ordinary places, in simple and unlikely ways, and when they do appear, they are unforgettable. The impression with which they left me was firm, and this is how the angels always work. The holy angels begin something in us and beckon us further, serving as our guardians on the way.

The angels I saw did not leave me with any immediate answers to the perplexing problems of life or thunder forth with a vocational call. They did not prevent my mom from dying four years later. They did not turn me into a world champion first-baseman like I had wished, or magically turn all my grades into As. But their presence was insistent. They simply extended an invitation that has not left me alone since that day. This book is the response to that invitation. It is a book about looking for and meeting angels.

These pages are about all angels — both the good angels who are obedient to God, and the evil angels who refused to obey Him. The last thing that the good angels would want is a book only about them. In their humility, they always point to God, not to themselves. The good angels shun the worldly spotlight. We only find them in unlikely, unexpected places, and in order to find them, we need to drag our eyes away from our own expectations. The holy angels were created good by God and permanently chose holiness. They long to do the will of God, and thus they seek to assist us on the way to salvation and to lead us in the path of divine grace so that we will enjoy eternal life with God in heaven.

The evil angels would also not want a book about them, but out of deceit rather than out of humility. They hide from us in order to conceal their assaults against us. They were created in holiness, but rejected God and forever fell from goodness. The bad angels are the demons. Having permanently lost their place in heaven by their own free choice against God, the evil angels now conspire to attack us — to destroy the beauty of the human being created in the image and likeness of God. The evil angels disguise themselves to appear beautiful because they want to destroy beauty, especially the beauty of the human soul. Their ultimate goal is to lead us into mortal sin and to make us impenitent in that choice so that we, like them, will lose heaven forever.

The good and evil angels are engaged in an ongoing battle, and we are drawn into that combat. In fact, the patristic scholar Cardinal Jean Daniélou, SJ, remarks that, "[A] battle is fought over every single man. Christ and his servants the angels are on one side, the princes of this world and their servants on the other."[3] In the course of this battle, each of us is led into a scarce and unfamiliar wilderness. The good angels are our guardians in the night, protecting us in the wilderness and teaching us asceticism. They guide us in virtue and protect us from the temptation of the evil angels, who seek to lure us into sin.[4] The night of this world can be quite dark, but the good angels protect us and help us to turn away the assaults of the evil angels. As we meet the holy angels, they uncover for us the path to humility — and to Christ. The good angels bring the light of Christ that conquers darkness, but darkness does not give up easily. It fights to keep its place.

When we face darkness, we need good friends. The great saints had long and close friendships with the good angels,[5] and we also need the friendship and powerful assistance of the good angels if we are to live a holy life. This friendship protects us from the shrewd snares and clever deceptions of the bad angels. It also heals us from the effects of previous sinful choices we have made.

We are not alone. In the holy angels, God has given us special helpers who work, usually behind the scenes, to teach, guide, and protect us. The good angels are our guardians in the night, who train us in the ways of light and protect us in the spiritual wilderness. They train us not with just any light, but with the light of Jesus Christ, the Son of God, risen and glorified.

If we are going to find the angels, then we have to do a little searching, especially in Scripture. St. Gregory the Great tells us,

"Nearly every page of Scripture testifies to the existence of angels and archangels."[6] Scripture also points us to those who have reflected on its mysteries. So, we will make appeal in our search to the writing of the Church Fathers, the saints, and also key theologians. Finally, our search will draw from the *Catechism of the Catholic Church,* either by direct quotation or reference to the section number in parenthetical notation.

The first part of this book considers the good angels as messengers of light, and as the first scientists. In the first chapter, we will learn how to locate the angels by resetting our expectations about where to look. We often look in the wrong places for angels, mistaking them for mythological characters in old-fashioned fables or spry New Age sprites. This chapter recalls an ancient meeting with God and His angels from the Book of Job that helps us find the angels.

Chapter two narrows the search for angels and considers their task as humble messengers by contrasting the modern messaging systems with the historical notion of a messenger. This leads to a treatment of angels as "pure spirits" and what invisibility means for angels (and for us!). Chapter two concludes with what happens when angels surrender (without defeat): They become visible and can even interact with human beings.

Chapter three takes up the topic of the creation of the angels in the Book of Genesis. The angels are created by God in a multitude that cannot be counted by human numbering systems. They are a gift of God's supernatural light, both reflecting that light, and at the same time, camouflaged within it. From that incandescent vantage point, they probe the wonder of creation such that they are, in a way, the first scientists.

In the second part of the book, we will examine the fallen angels who rejected God. Chapter four traces the origin of evil not to God, but to Lucifer and the fallen angels in their unlimited fury. Lucifer was the Bearer of Light, meant to cast light on the highest of God's mysteries. But in his pride, he rebelled, as is witnessed throughout Scripture, especially in the temptation of Our Lord in the desert. This chapter shows how Lucifer's sin is permanent, as is his envy of human beings made in the image of God.

Chapter five shows how the fallen angels attack human beings, especially through temptation and sin. The devil's temptations are disguised to attract us at first, inducing what we call a "spiritual hypothermia." An ancient warning from the Book of Genesis alerts us to beware of the ways with which he seeks to snare us in our thinking through temptation's thorny circuitry.

Chapter six takes us through five principal lies the devil uses to lure us into temptation. His lies are not only untruths, but they are like the coils of a great serpent by which he wants to ensnare us.

Faced with the darkness of temptation and sin, we realize how badly we need guardians. Part three of this book considers the good angels as our guardians in the night who protect us in the spiritual wilderness, lead us to meet the risen Christ, and guard us in our mission of following and serving Him.

Chapter seven examines how the good angels are our allies in the night of the spiritual life. As such, this chapter considers how the Cherubim with the flaming sword, who guards the way to the Tree of Life, casts the protective light throughout Scripture. The light in the darkness is the way the holy angels guide us in the wilderness of our spiritual journey.

Chapter eight shows us how the good angels are our guardians in the night who protect us in the spiritual wilderness. The Cherub with the flaming sword, who guards the way to the Garden of Eden after Adam and Eve's fall, sends forth a light that guides us in the way of humility. This chapter looks to five angels — the angel of humility, the angel of the ordinary, the angel of accompaniment, the angel of silence, and the angel of forgiveness — who free us from the coils of the devil.

Chapter nine examines two scenes from the Gospels, as Jesus confronts demons in the Gerasene district and in the synagogue at Capernaum.

Chapter ten reflects on the angels at Jesus' empty tomb and the angel who appears in St. Peter's prison cell in the Book of Acts. As the angels reveal the light of the Risen Lord, they lead us in the Lord's work and continue to protect us against evil.

It is hoped that you will take from these pages a renewed awareness of the crucial place of the angels in the plan of God. Throughout these chapters, you will rediscover the work of the angels in the Old Testament and the New Testament, and be able to perceive the work of the good angels in our own wildernesses, wherever and whatever these may be. The good angels know their way, and they long to be our friends — to teach, guide, and protect us. As St. Clement said, "Let us look carefully at the whole host of His angels; they stand ready and serve His will."[7] May you follow the trail of the angels through these pages and be led to a deeper friendship with the good and holy angels. May their friendship and ministry lead you to intimacy with Jesus Christ, Lord and Savior forever.

PART I

THE GOOD ANGELS:
Messengers of Light

Chapter One

FOCUSING ON ANGELS

What light is to the eye, angels are to the soul. Light and angels are both messengers. Sunlight carries the beauty of a mountain stream to our eyes. Light from a lamp carries the words on this page to your eyes. Light allows us to see the wooden bookshelf across the room, the soft chair by the window, the flowering meadow at the entrance of the park. St. Hilary even says, "Our eyes cannot fulfill their task without light."[1] Certain lasting human friendships have what seems to be a natural light of trust that allows us to know another person so thoroughly. Natural light in all its variety is important. Angels work with light as well — the supernatural light of the revelation of God.

The angels uncover for us the deep mysteries of God. As natural light makes things known in our physical world, the angels make known the supernatural light of God's glory in which they were created. Natural light reveals mysteries to the eye. Similarly, angels reflect a brilliant light that eludes and overcomes worldly obstacles of time and circumstance, so that we can internalize knowledge and affection for the mysteries of God — and so come to trust Him. But we may need years to discover and learn the deeper meaning of what we see in that reflected light. Light reveals the beauty of the flowers in the meadow, but we need time to learn about photosynthesis and the way the flowers grow. The familiar smile of a lasting friend reveals someone who knows and loves us, but it has taken years to let down the defenses, sustain the hard knocks of life together, and see each other through to forgiveness and acceptance.

Angels can reveal things to the soul immediately, but we often need time to understand and grasp the meaning of the profound mysteries they reveal, such as the mystery of our calling in this life, the mystery of love, and the painful mystery of loss. The angels don't make the mysteries of God known in such a way that we figure everything out or "solve" the divine mysteries, but so that we are led further into these mysteries and to union with God. Angels are patient messengers as they guide us, kindly adapting their genius to our speed.

Three Mistakes We Make about Angels

It is easy — and potentially dangerous — to make mistakes about angels, as these mistakes can throw us off the path to union with God. The good angels are faithful, pure spirits; real beings, whose mission is to make known our path to union with God in the spiritual life. If we make mistakes about angels, we can miss the beauty of Christ and the nature of the Christian call. We will likely also end up on the wrong path, just going around in circles in the spiritual life. There are three common mistakes that we can make about angels, and these can lead us to give up on them, and miss their tremendous friendship in the spiritual life. But we can avoid these mistakes if we anticipate them, so that we can encounter the angels more easily and be led to the beauty of Christ.

The first mistake is to see angels as fairy tale creatures who roam through kindly fables as old-fashioned, powerful presences. In this view, angels are seen as mythical creatures who were once cast in supporting roles in the Bible, but whom modern science has now explained away. This way of giving up on the angels only allows them to step out of their forced retirement once a year, so they may take their tame place, confined as background silver silhouettes against a dark navy night sky on Christmas cards, or for a cameo in a Christmas carol. But, as we shall see, angels are far more than a seasonal decoration.

The second mistake about angels is to treat them as a lyrical or poetic expression of internal psychological inspirations.[2] This view dresses the angels up as New Age sprites, who flit behind the scenes of life as little more than anonymous eclectic energy forces. It recasts the angels as celestial personality coaches who help us find the "divine spark" hidden within us. Finding this "spark" supposedly helps us to advance our prosperity and enhance our personality. But the holy angels will not be domesticated by our expectations. Just as angels are far more than a holiday ornament, they are far more formidable than a spiritual fad.

The third mistake about angels is the one Christians tend to make. It is to expect (or to demand) things from the angels that we should not expect of them. We want them to swoop into our lives, like celestial superheroes arriving from out-of-nowhere at precisely the right moment — at the death–bed to save our loved one from cancer, or a split second before a car crash to prevent the terrible accident. In addition to averting tragedy, we want them to help us get what we want — to whisper the winning lottery numbers in our ear as we fill out the lotto slip, to give us the answers on a test, or to get the vacation weather just right.

We want angels to override the laws of nature and rearrange those rules so that things turn out to our good fortune, no matter what the circumstance. When they deliver as we expect, our belief in their existence becomes a type of reward for their good behavior. When they do not deliver as we expect, we are disappointed and think angels cannot be real. Our expectations of the angels do not place a burden on the angels; our expectations place a burden on *us*. Our expectations can be so heavy that they can crush us.[3] And, given the beauty the angels want to reveal to us, that is a big burden to place on ourselves.

What's the danger with these mistakes, especially the one Christians tend to make? The danger is that we overlook the mysterious work of the good angels, because we are busy looking for something else, some other result or outcome. And there is a deeper danger still. If our expectations so dominate our lives, the evil angel Lucifer, and the fallen angels who followed him, will leap to pretend to fulfill our expectations. Lucifer *wants* us to forget about the good angels, to make mistakes about them. This clears the way for his insidious temptation to assault us without the protection of the good and holy angels.

Here's another reason why our false expectations are such a danger: No matter how understandable or seemingly beneficial, our false expectations encourage pride. Pride often takes the form of us demanding what we want, of getting our expectations met quickly and on our terms. Lucifer thrives on pride. When he detects a false expectation, even an apparently good one, he puts on his working gloves and seeks to sow division and bitterness between us and God.

He does this through lies, deception, and illusion. He obscures our awareness of the simple beauty, gifts, and blessings that we do have, repeatedly telling us that we do not measure up or fit in. He simultaneously presents to us an illusion of what we "should" be, to such an extent that we loathe the former and lust after the non-existent latter. He coaxes us to expend so much energy pressuring ourselves and others to chase the glitter of the illusion, as we continually bypass the beauty of the real.

For him, expectations are the raw material of pride and vanity, a key ingredient in his sad and busy workshop. But, even here, when we feel that our pride and vanity are like an avalanche, the good and holy angels assist us, protect and guard us, showing us the path away from our expectations toward the way of humility and reliance on the providence of God. When we show even the slightest sign of humility — and of relying on the providence of God — we will find the angels ... or rather, they will find us.

What to Expect from the Angels

Here's the good news. Even if we make mistakes about the angels, they don't make mistakes about us. If we expect from them what we shouldn't expect, they don't reject us. They know us and love us. Even if we give up on the angels, they never give up on us. They give a lot more thought to our existence than most of us give to theirs.

Angels do swoop in, though not in the ways we often expect. Angels untangle our expectations and help to realign them to the providence of God. The angels can do this because they are closer to us than even our own expectations. The angels therefore teach us to rely not on our own expectations, but on God's providence. God's providence is not a blank check or a painkiller. It is far more. Angels teach us about this "more." God uses the holy angels to dispose us to His providence. They bring us to goodness and seek to guard us from evil.[4]

It often takes the good angels a long time to help us trust in God's providence rather than insist on the fulfillment of our own expectations. Given that we easily and often wrap our will around ourselves and what we want, it can take a long time for the angels to get through to us. But they are persistent. Letting go of our own expectations and our pride feels like a defeat for us, but it is the most sublime of victories.

The holy angels do not serve our pride, but our good. They do not count on happy endings as the world defines them, or the happy endings we expect. Angels count only on the Son of God. They count on Christ's victory over sin and death and His revelation of the Father's love. Angels intervene to make known the mystery of Christ and, in doing so, to save souls. And they often do so right in the middle of horrible disease and terrible accidents. But as they intervene to make known Christ and His mysteries, they do not try to meet our specific expectations, desperately as we may want them to do so. They have something much deeper in mind. After all, there is a battle going on.

The Angels Are in a Meeting — and Satan Shows Up

The Book of Job contains the record of a meeting between God and the angels — the good angels and one bad angel. From that simple list of those present, before even a word is spoken, a contrast is clear.

As the meeting begins, the "sons of God" come to station themselves with God in His presence (Job 1:6). The fifth-century Church Father Hesychius of Jerusalem explains that this is a meeting of the angels who had been sent to serve human beings.[5] St. Gregory the Great tells us that "sons of God" refers to the good angels.[6] The Hebrew word for "station themselves" does not simply mean that the angels stood near God. It means that they live permanently in His presence, forever confirmed in goodness and grace.

After God and the angels gather, a mysterious other one also arrives. It is Satan. St. Gregory tells us that Satan is the evil angel, "he who had a long time before been damned and banished from their number."[7] Satan was Lucifer, the angel who disobeyed God and took one-third of the angels with him when he fell from heaven (Rv 12:4, 9).[8] That phrase "also arrives" is important. It implies a deep theological truth. This phrase, in the original language of Scripture, implies that Satan not only arrives separately from the holy angels, but also that he arrives *in contradiction* to them. His presence in the conversation is of a different sort than theirs. Satan is not in heaven. He does not "stand near God" as the angels do, but he presents himself so as *to separate* those who stand with and remain close to God on earth. Satan arrives to insert a rift, a division.

He wants this division to give rise to a disunity that destroys everything it touches, even God's providence and plan. We see this in Scripture and in human history. The Synoptic Gospels (Matthew, Mark, and Luke), the New Testament scholar Heinrich Schlier explains, "confirm the tendency of the satanic power to be the distortion, thwarting, ruin, annihilation and undoing of creation."[9] The Catholic theologian Hans Urs von Balthasar points out the evil influence that has sparked the terrible devastation and annihilations throughout recent history: "Everywhere, beside Faust, beside Hegel, Marx, Lenin, Stalin, beside Zarathustra and Hitler, we discern the shadow of a demon, insinuating that all that exists 'deserves to be destroyed.'"[10]

The contrast builds as the conversation of the meeting proceeds. God immediately directs His attention to Satan. The Lord asks him, "Whence have you come?" (Jb 1:7, RSV). This is more than a simple question. The Hebrew word for "whence" is almost identical to the word meaning "nothing," "no," or "no longer." God is reminding Satan that Satan comes from a "no," from a refusal, from the nothingness of a lie.

By His question, God condemns Satan's ways, because having said "no" to God, Satan cannot receive the light of truth.[11] Lucifer's "no" to God was not a simple refusal, after which he fell from heaven. His "no" to God was a permanent "no" that *continually* seeks to undo God's creation. Satan's ultimate desire is nothingness, achieved through disobedience. God reminds Satan of his disobedience and his evil desire.

Satan responds to God's question: "From going to and fro on the earth, and from walking up and down on it" (Jb 1:7, RSV). This means, St. Gregory says, that Satan has been searching for grounds on which to accuse human beings.[12] Satan's going "to and fro" is his frantic attempt to snatch away from us our knowledge of God's goodness and replace it with his own lies. He accuses us by his lies and seeks to sabotage us with one persuasive temptation after another. As St. Peter will make clear, "Your opponent the devil is prowling around like a roaring lion looking for [someone] to devour" (1 Pt 5:8). Satan always attempts to spread his nothingness "on the earth" because he detests God's creation.

At this point, the topic of demonic possession captures our attention. While demonic possession is possible, the devil seems to prefer to work through temptation, rather than the more dramatic possession. He wants to blend in, like covert operatives deep undercover spreading disinformation, so that we think evil is the way things ought to be. Operating mainly by possession would be like invading with an army. That would drive Christians and others to the Church for protection. Satan prefers to use his fallen angelic intellect to lure us into rejecting God — without us immediately realizing the danger of what we are doing. Today, the most widespread reaction to the devil is not even skepticism, but outright denial of his existence and influence in our world. Evil today "has been watered down to a series of dangerous repressions within the personality"[13] that, when acted upon, result in tragedy and violence. With evil watered down, the devil's existence is negated. That is just as he would want it. As we discern the devil's subtlety, we realize more and more how crucial it is that we not only cling to Christ through the sacraments, prayer, and the ways of virtue; it is vital that we turn to the holy angels who long to guide us to Christ and His grace-filled protection.

Notice that, already in this early conversation, Satan brings his devouring ways *even* to this gathering of the "sons of God." God asks Satan a question: "Whence have you come?" God asks the question not for Satan's benefit, but for ours. God raises this question to protect us from Satan's power by reminding us of Satan's fall — that in choosing disobedience to God, Satan chose the nothingness of sin, and that if we listen to Satan and choose sin, we will be choosing nothingness. By His question, God already seeks to give us arms by which we might ask Christ to dislodge Satan from any ground he has sought to gain in our heart. The holy angels are our allies who guide us more deeply to Christ.

Guardians Surround, but Satan Complains

The meeting continues. God asks Satan a second question: "Have you considered my servant Job, that there is none like him on the earth, a blameless and upright man, who fears God and turns away from evil?" (Jb 1:8, RSV). From the context, it seems that God had been speaking to the good angels about the virtues of Job before Satan arrived. Notice that God refers to Job as "my servant," thus emphasizing that Satan is *not* God's servant. It is as if God is saying, "After all you did to Adam and Eve and their descendants, have you considered Job?"

The Hebrew for "considered" doesn't simply ask Satan if he has taken note of Job. The word literally means: *Have you been able to lay a violent hand upon the heart of Job?* The literal translation gives us a hint at what is really going on: Satan has been trying to attack Job *and has been* unable. Remember that God was talking to the good angels about Job. Their conversation "surrounded" Job. In the spiritual sense, their conversation was the deeper place from which the protection of Job emerged. Satan interrupts the conversation precisely because he cannot get what he wants: the ability to attack Job and try to separate him from God. He wants to disrupt the guardians who protect Job.

As usual, when Satan is unable to do something, he lies. And he usually phrases his lie as a question. In the Garden of Eden, as we will explore in detail later, Satan began his temptation of Eve with the question, "Did God really say ... ?" (Gn 3:1). And so, Satan responds to God's question and says, "Is it for nothing that Job is God-fearing? Have you not surrounded him and his family and all that he has with your protection?" (Jb 1:9–10). Satan complains about the protection God gives to human beings. St. Gregory the Great assures us, "The old enemy is enraged against the righteous the more he perceives that they are hedged around by the favor of God's protection."[14] The lie Satan inserts is that Job fears God because of the protection afforded Job. Satan cunningly suggests that God plays favorites, that God has bought Job off with divine favors — heavenly bribes. (Even here, Satan must implicitly praise Job, noting that he has not acquired his wealth by means of injustice.[15])

But, more central to our purposes, Satan complains about the *guardian* angels. The *Catechism of the Catholic Church* teaches that, "From its beginning until death human life is surrounded by their watchful care and intercession" (336). The guardian angels "become intermediaries between God and man, as they lay our needs and our fears before Him, offering God our desires and our prayers, and in return they bring us His grace and His gifts."[16] St. Thomas teaches that each human being has an angel deputed to guard him or her.[17] Lucifer detests the guardian angels, because of who they are, but also because they are effective. Drawing on the power of Christ, they thwart Satan's attempts to harm our souls. Notice that while Satan "roams" the earth, God's protecting angels also purposefully march forth. Satan doesn't have the world to himself. If he operates like an undercover agent, the angels also operate behind the scenes to protect us from him.

In Hebrew, the word Satan uses to describe the protection afforded to Job means that Job is protected on every side. The guardian angels encircle, surround, and encompass God's servant. They protect us for eternal salvation. They guard us from the assaults of the devil and enable us to live the moral life. This is why it is important that we avoid those three mistakes about angels we discussed earlier.

Furthermore, this encircling protection is not just a bubble or perimeter of safety around Job. The "encircling" of the guardian angels creates a momentum that assists Job, that propels his "turn[ing] away" (Jb 1:8, RSV) from evil. To put it another way, the guardian angels create a wave of virtue that we can step into freely and be preserved. Satan attempts to interrupt, disturb, and destroy this wave. He can only disrupt it by lying, which is why he wages war on virtue by lies.

Why is this ancient meeting and the old interruption so important? The story helps us to locate the good angels: behind enemy lines and behind the scenes.

The Angels: Behind Enemy Lines

Job is in a battle that Satan is waging against God. So are we. Balthasar noted: "The Christian is not fighting with adversaries of the same order and on the same level as himself: he is part of God's front, bears his weaponry and is fighting alongside God in a campaign against his sworn enemies."[18] Jean Daniélou, has likewise made clear that "The drama of mankind is unfolded in the context of a wider conflict, between the spiritual Powers that hold men captive, and the angels of God under the kingship of Christ."[19]

The first place to look for the angels is behind enemy lines, where we are. Because of the Fall of Adam and Eve, human beings are born with original sin and in a fallen world. Baptism takes away original sin, but we are still in a fallen world — though strengthened for the spiritual battle. The baptized are blessed warriors, but are still behind enemy lines in this world. The devil wants us to think we are here alone, on our own, that God has abandoned us. If we do think of God, the devil would have us believe that unless we can prove ourselves to God by perfect prayer or a flawless moral life, then God will have nothing to do with us, so why even try. But God doesn't abandon us. While we are down behind enemy lines, we are not there alone. We are not without allies.

We see this in the dramatic stories of angelic protection and rescue. Angels close the mouths of the ferocious beasts as Daniel stands in the lions' den: "My God sent his angel and closed the lions' mouths so that they have not hurt me" (Dn 6:23). Angels rescue Lot from the destruction of Sodom (see Gn 19:1–11). They carry out the tenth plague in Egypt (Ex 12). The angels strengthen Elijah (1 Kgs 19:5–7), and save the three Hebrews from the fire (Dn 3:25, 49). An angelic army assists Elisha (2 Kgs 6:15ff). An angel kills the Assyrians (2 Kgs 19:35) in the Old Testament, and Herod in the New (Acts 12:23). An angel delivers St. Peter from prison (Acts 12:7). The angels minister to the Lord Jesus after His time in the wilderness (Mt 4:11). Angels know how to handle dire situations. They have seen them before.

We can say that angels are God's extraction team. They break us out, free us; they know the way to freedom in Christ. That is humility. Humility confounds the devil and blinds him. As we fight alongside God, the good angels are our constant and unseen allies in the battle. They are always with us, down behind enemy lines. God's messengers know how to blend in. Especially when they're working behind enemy lines.

The Angels: Behind the Scenes

While the angels are down behind enemy lines, they're also found behind the scenes. In the Bible, we sometimes see them operate in the open. In addition to the events already mentioned, three angels appear to the childless Abraham to reveal that he will be the father of a great nation (see Gn 22:15–18), and initiate him into the secrets of God.[20] An angel reveals to the mother of Samson that she will conceive a son (Jgs 13:3). Most famously, an angel repeatedly appears to St. Joseph in dreams, to tell him what to do in his role as the foster father of the Savior (Mt 1:20–21; 2:13).

We also find in the Bible that the angels work along the back-channel corridors of life, just beyond the obvious. One example takes place as the Lord is on His way to Samaria. St. Luke notes that Jesus "sent messengers ahead of him. On the way they entered a Samaritan village to prepare for his reception there" (Lk 9:52). We know that God often sends angels ahead of Him, to make ready his way, and that He fulfills that which His messengers announce (see Is 44:26).

Who are these messengers? St. Luke can mean that Jesus sent human disciples ahead of Him to make the practical arrangements for His visit to the village. The words can also mean that the Lord sent His holy angels.[21] The original Greek word for "messengers" comes from the Hebrew word *mal' ak,* meaning "angel." The angels wouldn't be preparing the practical realities of His passing through, but going to make ready the hearts of those He was going to visit. The readying of hearts involves a behind-the-scenes effort.

A second example is the pool of Bethesda. We are told that the waters of the pool are stirred by an angel: "For [from time to time] an angel of the Lord used to come down into the pool; and the water was stirred up, so the first one to get in [after the stirring of the water] was healed of whatever disease afflicted him" (Jn 5:4). The angel is "behind the scenes," and causes the stirring of the water. Later tradition identifies this angel as the Archangel Raphael, the angel of healing. The ones seeking healing do not necessarily see the angel, but only the commotion caused in the water by his presence.

A third example is when the three youths, Shadrach, Meshach, and Abednego, defy the order of King Nebuchadnezzar to worship the golden statue that the king had set up (see Dn 3:14). Once the three youths are cast into the fire as a penalty, it is the king himself who sees a fourth man in the fire who looks like a "son of God" (3:92). The king then affirms that God had sent His angel to deliver His servants who trusted in Him (3:95). The angel creates no fanfare, but acts behind the scenes at the most desperate moment to save the three youths.

The angels know how to operate behind the scenes. It is a sign of their humility. Humility blends in. Humility and angels go hand-in-hand.

Chapter Two

HUMBLE MESSENGERS

The good angels can work behind enemy lines and behind the scenes because they are pure spirits. They are invisible messengers of humility. They know the importance of the message, and they know the terrible threat that the message is under.

It is easy today to take messages and messengers for granted. We receive dozens of email and text messages a day. We live in a time of long-range, instant communication. In the ancient world, the world depended on the work of human messengers who had to endure perilous journeys of weeks, months, and even years to make things known from one person or community to another. Messengers were highly valued. They did not just carry things from one place to another; they functioned as intermediaries between the sender of the message and the intended receiver. They often carried highly confidential and valuable information. Delivering the message could mean the difference between life and death.

Reliable messages required having reliable messengers. Not just anyone could be a messenger. He had to be someone close to the sender, someone trusted and brave. The messenger had to be so trusted, because he served as a kind of *substitute* for the sender. He was vested with something of the sender's authority, and he quickly became a target of the leader's enemies. The messenger had to avoid calling attention to himself. He had to blend in. The first attribute of the messenger was his humility. He had to be humble enough to work behind the scenes. The angels' work — the work God created them to do — can be said to be a work of humility. They serve God, asking nothing for themselves, doing nothing to put themselves forward. Unlike Satan and the fallen angels, the good angels obey God — without a second thought, we might say.

Humility makes them little enough to carry a limitless message. It allows them to work behind the scenes, get out of the way and stand for another, to make their own another's message. Humility and invisibility have a lot in common.

Angels as Pure Spirits

Henri-Marie Boudon emphasizes that angels "have often been invisibly present" as they visit us.[1] To say that angels are invisibly present means that they are very near to us, are with us, though we cannot detect their presence with our five physical senses. In fantasy stories or science fiction films, a hero or villain can become invisible temporarily due to the special power of a magical ring, a potion, or a cloak of invisibility. In this case, invisibility is a form of stealth camouflage that gives the hero or villain better odds of escaping a difficult predicament unscathed, or even overpowering a foe. That is a superficial meaning of invisibility. There is nothing superficial about angels. The angels become visible and invisible, but not as a divine trick of a heavenly superhero that is meant to convince someone to believe in God. Their invisibility is not fantasy, fiction, or illusion. It is real.

Invisibility does not mean that the angels are absent. It often means they are present. Angels are invisible because they are pure spirits. St. Thomas Aquinas refers to a verse in Psalm 104 to describe angels as pure spirits: "You make the winds your messengers" (Ps 104:4). (The author of the Letter to the Hebrews refers to this psalm as well in speaking of the angels [see 1:7]). St. Thomas thinks this passage is more properly translated as "He makes His angels [messengers] spirits," that is, incorporeal creatures — immaterial, intellectual creatures — whom God creates.[2] The *Catechism of the Catholic Church* affirms that "The existence of the spiritual, non-corporeal beings that Sacred Scripture usually calls 'angels' is a truth of faith. The witness of Scripture is as clear as the unanimity of Tradition" (328).

To say angels are "pure spirits" does not mean that they are ghosts, apparitions, or phantoms. It especially does not mean that they are unreal. They *are* real. To refer to angels as "pure spirits" means that angels are a special kind of being — a real personal being created by God with free will and intellect, without a body composed of matter.[3] They are purely spiritual beings who are part of the invisible, but nonetheless real, creation. As such, they are present in and work within the visible world, but do so in such a way that they are not confined by laws that govern physical bodies in time and space. Their nature as pure spirits allows the angels to transcend the laws of time and space, and not be seen or restricted in the way a physical body would be.[4] Their nature as pure spirits even allows them to become visible in our dreams.

As pure spirits, the angels act with incredible speed, such that "in an instant, they can pass from one end of the world to the other."[5] Think, for example, of the speed with which light fills a room when you turn on a light switch. Angels are quicker than that. The angels are intellectual creatures, which means they know intuitively the depths of the glory of God. They also know the tremendous light of the glory of God's presence, of His interior mysteries, and of His plan of divine providence.[6] They understand the way His glory is reflected throughout all of creation.

Angels know material things in a better way than human beings do. They participate in God's knowledge of all He has created, which they received from God in their creation. With this supernatural knowledge, angels, because they are pure spirits, can *intervene* in numerous ways, countless times a day, right in front of us, in a way we cannot detect with our five physical senses, though we can at times perceive their presence with our mind.

Angels can intervene because, as pure spirits, they have a distinctive relation to space. They enjoy the vision of God, yet they act on the earth as "ministering spirits" (Heb 1:14). J. R. R. Tolkien explains that our Guardian Angel faces "two ways" — to God and to us — and so can act with this astounding simultaneity.[7] Recall the words of Jesus: "See that you do not despise one of these little ones, for I say to you that their angels in heaven always look upon the face of my heavenly Father" (Mt 18:10). Their proximity to God *enhances*, rather than prevents, their simultaneous closeness to us. The angels are with God in heaven and are, *at the same time,* with us.

Thus the angels can fulfill the commands of God immediately on earth. Recall the experience of Abraham on Mount Moriah: "Then Abraham reached out and took the knife to slaughter his son. But the angel of the LORD called to him from heaven, 'Abraham, Abraham!' 'Here I am,' he answered. 'Do not lay your hand on the boy,' said the angel. 'Do not do the least thing to him. For now I know that you fear God'" (Gn 22:10-12). Recall also the story in 2 Samuel: "The angel of the Lord was then standing at the threshing floor of Araunah the Jebusite" when the Lord told him what to do (2 Sm 24:16). St. Thomas says that the angel, even while in heaven, knows what is happening to human beings and can be with us in an instant.[8] In this, the angels model for us in a unique way the fulfillment of the command to love God and neighbor (Mk 12:30–31).

Invisibility and Humility

The invisibility has a second, much deeper meaning. We might call it the "hidden meaning of invisibility," or its "spiritual meaning." Angelic invisibility is a sign of angelic humility. The angels' invisibility is not about *them*. It is about God. *Invisibility is simply the first way the angel points to God.* Pride demands to be seen. Pride calls attention to itself. It thrives on intrigue and seeks out drama. Pride is the enemy of the true messenger. It has the constant need to reassure itself that it is perfect.

The angels of God do not advertise themselves. Humility prefers to elude the spotlight and be invisible. Their invisibility arises not from their own power, but from their immersion into the humility of the Son of God. Their invisibility is the transparency of humility that gets out of the way and points always to Jesus Christ. The angels maneuver from this hidden space to reflect the supernatural light of Christ, so that He, and not they, become the saving focus.

Seen in this light, the invisibility of the angels is one of their first lessons to us. Humility is the invisibility of the Christian life. St. John the Baptist longed to be invisible. St. John says of Christ, "He must increase; I must decrease" (Jn 3:30). On the other hand, pride and ambition are the distorted visibility of the Christian life which wants to see and be seen as it seeks "places of honor" (Mk 12:39).

When Angels Show Themselves

Angels can surrender their invisibility and can even take on a physical body we can see, if that serves their mission. God can permit the angels to assume a corporeal body to assist us in benefiting from their companionship.[9] When they do so, the body they assume does not become part of the nature of the angel; it is an instrument to communicate in a visible way with human beings.[10] In the Bible, angels appear seemingly out of nowhere, and disappear just as quickly. St. Thomas says that this ability comes from a special grace of God.[11] St. Thomas gives the example of the angels who appeared to Abraham.[12] The angels assumed bodies for his benefit, so that they could converse with him in a way familiar to him.

The Bible tells numerous stories of angels appearing in bodily form. They often speak to people, like the angels who appeared to Abraham. Recall from the Book of Numbers: "Then the LORD opened Balaam's eyes, so that he saw the angel of the LORD standing on the road with sword drawn; and he knelt and bowed down to the ground" (Nm 22:31). An angel appears and speaks to Manoah and her husband to tell them of the conception and birth of Samson (see Jgs 13:3ff).

The angel, "one who looked like a man" (Dn 8:15; 10:5; see Ez 40:3), appears to the prophet Daniel and calls out with a human voice. But Daniel also learns the angel's name. Daniel attests to a visit from the angel Gabriel, in which he hears Gabriel speak:

> I was still praying, when the man, Gabriel, whom I had seen in vision before, came to me in flight at the time of the evening offering. He instructed me in these words: "Daniel, I have now come to give you understanding. When you began your petition, an answer was given which I have come to announce, because you are beloved." (Daniel 9:21–23)

We learn the names of angels at other times in Scripture. We learn the names of Michael (see Rv 12:7; Dn 10:13; 10:21; 12:1), and Raphael (Tb 12:15), in addition to Gabriel (Dn 8:16; 9:21; Lk 1:19). Michael is the archangel who defends us in battle. Raphael is the archangel of healing whom God sends to soothe and cure our pains, who also brings us comfort in affliction. Gabriel is the archangel who brings special messages from God.

The work of the angels often overlaps. For example, even as we ask for the Archangel Michael to defend us, it is often that we need healing from Raphael. We can be defended in a moment, in one fell swoop. Healing usually takes a lot longer. Tobit affirms that the Archangel Raphael not only appeared to him in human form, but also knew Tobit by name and knew the content of his prayer (see Tb 12:12–14). Not only is the Archangel Raphael the one who brings God's medicine of healing, but he also guided Tobit on his pilgrimage and travels. We are told, not just that the Archangel Gabriel appeared to Zechariah, but also where the angel stood: "at the right of the altar of incense" (Lk 1:11). Luke tells us that the whole assembly of people praying outside of the temple did not see the angel enter or depart (Lk 1:10ff).

As they did with Abraham, angels can make physical contact with things, animals, and even human beings. The angel who appeared to Gideon carried a staff by which he caused fire to consume the sacrifice (see Jgs 6:11–24). An angel closed the mouths of the lions threatening Daniel (Dn 6:23). Even the animals can recognize the presence of the angel: The donkey of Balaam turns off the road when it sees the angel (Nm 22:23–33) — when Balaam himself doesn't see him. Recall that when the prophet Elijah is afraid and flees for his life, God repeatedly sends an angel, who touches Elijah to wake and rouse him from his fearful flight, and to nourish him for the journey (1 Kgs 19:5–7).

Other times, angels appear in bodily form, but those to whom they appear don't realize it is an angel before them. This must have been common enough that the author of the Letter to the Hebrews saw it as important to offer the general counsel: "Do not neglect hospitality, for through it some have unknowingly entertained angels" (Heb 13:2).

Still, at other times, angels appear, and the people to whom they appear only gradually realize the angelic presence.

> While Joshua was near Jericho, he raised his eyes and saw one who stood facing him, drawn sword in hand. Joshua went up to him and asked, "Are you one of us or one of our enemies?" He replied, "Neither. I am the commander of the army of the LORD: now I have come." Then Joshua fell down to the ground in worship, and said to him, "What has my lord to say to his servant?" The commander of the army of the LORD replied to Joshua, "Remove your sandals from your feet, for the place on which you are standing is holy." (Joshua 5:13–15)

Similarly, an angel appears in the Acts of the Apostles to a Gentile, telling him to send someone to St. Peter. The Gentile explained "how he had seen [the] angel standing in his house, saying, 'Send someone to Joppa and summon Simon, who is called Peter, who will speak words to you by which you and all your household will be saved'" (Acts 11:13-14). Later, in Acts, St. Paul has a vision during the night of a man of Macedonia who pleads with him, saying: "Come over to Macedonia and help us" (Acts 16:9). Origen explains that the man of Macedonia is actually an angel meant to lead the pagan peoples to God.[13]

The Marvel of Invisibility

The angels' invisibility is more a marvel than their occasional visibility. Angels intervene and act in our world far more often with a personal and invisible presence than they do with a visible presence.[14] Humility is so much a part of their mission that the humility of the angels *is* their abiding style. It is the precondition of all else that they proclaim. They show us that humility is unlimited littleness that creates room for Another — Christ.

True humility *loves* to go unnoticed. It is so central to the angels that even their creation is hidden, camouflaged in an otherwise incandescent light. It is to the creation of the angels that we now turn.

Chapter Three

THE CREATION OF THE ANGELS AND THE ANGELS OF CREATION

From the examination of their invisibility and visibility, and their interaction with the created world and human beings, additional key considerations immediately arise as we consider the angels. This chapter will examine how angels are "down to earth" — that is, the moment of their creation, their role as mediators of the light of God's glory, their number, and finally, their mission to teach us, protect us, and to guide creation.

We will first consider the moment of their creation. When did God create the angels? The second consideration is their number. How many angels did God create? The Fathers of the Church point us to the Book of Genesis as we begin to consider these two questions. Having responded to these two questions, we can then consider better the work of the angels of creation.

God the Father's first words in Scripture are a simple sentence of only four words: "Let there be light" (Gn 1:3). They are said out of the superabundance of divine love. There is a lot more to this original light than we usually think.

The light that God the Father calls forth with His first words is not the solar light of the sun. It is not the lunar light of the moon. Nor is it the guiding light of the stars. Those lights are created on the fourth day of creation (see Gn 1:16ff). The mysterious glow of the light of the first day is a far more luminous and incandescent light than those natural kinds of light.

St. Augustine tells us that when God says, "Let there be light," He creates the entire multitude of the heavenly host of angels.[1] St. Basil the Great agrees that with these simple words, God creates "rational and invisible natures, and the whole orderly arrangement of spiritual creatures. ... These fill completely the essence of the invisible world."[2] "No sooner were they made, than they were made light," St. Augustine says.[3] They are so close to God, who "is light" (1 Jn 1:5), that their first name in all of Scripture is "light." The psalmist speaks of the creation of the angels when he speaks of the creation of the "great lights" (Ps 136:7). The Book of Baruch speaks of the angels when it says that God "sends out the lightning, and it goes, calls it, and trembling it obeys him" (Bar 3:33). God's light is no ordinary light. It is supernatural. His "light" is another name for His glory: His overflowing beauty, goodness, and providence. The angels come forth in obedience to the providence of God, who is "the Father of lights" (Jas 1:17).

God brings into existence all the heavenly host of angels on the first day of creation. The theologian Louis Bouyer says that the angels are created prior to the visible world, and are superior to it.[4] Out of all other creatures, the angels are nearest to God and resemble him the most.[5] The psalmist tells us that the angels are so close to God that they are His very throne: "He is enthroned on the cherubim" (Ps 99:1, see also 18:10; Dn 3:55). The Book of Revelation speaks of seven angels "who stood before God" (8:2, see also 4:5). Micaiah says that he "saw the LORD seated on his throne, with the whole host of heaven standing to his right and to his left"

(1 Kgs 22:19). Pope St. John Paul II explains that reference to the angels as the "throne of God" shows the maximum closeness of the angels to God.[6] The angels are very close to Him, and reflect the light of His glory. The power of God's light-filled word of the first day of creation is so magnificent that it calls into existence an uncountable host of angels. The angels are the first creatures made by God, and are the first revelation of His goodness and beauty.[7] Light is God's first miracle. As such, God entrusts to the angels a special ministry in regard to human beings.

Out of the depths of His magnificent love, God wants to share His glory with us human beings. He wants to be close to us. Yet God does not force the light of His closeness on us. As free beings, we are invited to accept His light and offered the grace to stand within it. The brilliant radiance of God's glory is unapproachable and awesome in itself. If He were to share it directly with the human soul, or if we were to approach it directly, its tremendous splendor would overwhelm and annihilate us. He must give us not only His light, but also the grace to stand within that light. The way God has chosen to extend this grace to us and the ability to stand within it is through the ministry of angels.

The angels are especially suited for this task of mediating the light of God's glory to us. The psalmist tells us that the angels carry out the work of God and do His will: "Bless the LORD, all you his angels, mighty in strength, acting at his behest, obedient to his command. Bless the LORD, all you his hosts, his ministers who carry out his will" (Ps 103:20–21). Sirach concurs: "For him each messenger succeeds, and at his bidding accomplishes his will" (Sir 43:26).

The Angels in the Light of God

The angels convey God's light to us. How can they do this? It is because of the kind of creature God created them to be. Their nearness to God means that the angels, in the moment of their creation, knew God in the supernatural light of His glorious role as their Creator.[8] Angels have the strength to stand before the overwhelming light of His glory. Recall the words of the Archangel Gabriel to Zechariah: "'I am Gabriel, who stand before God" (Lk 1:19). Likewise, the Book of Sirach says, "God has given his hosts the strength to stand firm before his glory" (Sir 42:17).

After the Resurrection of Jesus, the angels at the empty tomb appear in "dazzling garments" (Lk 24:4), and "clothed in a white robe" (Mk 16:5), because they reflect the glory of the Resurrection.[9]

Likewise, "the glory of the Lord shone around" the shepherds as the angels appeared (see Lk 2:9). The angels there reflect the light of the Incarnation of the Son of God, born of Mary. The shepherds are terrified at the brilliant light. Unlike the angels, they cannot stand before it on their own. The angels, by their message, transform the terror into holy fear, and guide the shepherds to Christ, sharing with them the grace of God by which they can enter the tremendous mystery.

This does not mean that angels are divine, or semi-divine. They are not "little gods." The angels do not substitute for God. Nor do they replace or fill in for Him. Nor do they know Him in His deepest substance. They are real, spiritual creatures who reflect the divine light. John Scotus Eriugena, the 9th century Irish theologian teaches that the angels are light in the sense that they are a perceptible presence that draws human beings to God.[10]

But they are also not idle spectators or celestial bystanders in anything that God does. God engages the angels, and they engage us. He wants to be so close to us that He makes use of the angels to carry on His intimate interactions with us. They stand before His glory to worship Him and to communicate that glory to us. They communicate His glory by reflecting His supernatural light. It is an invitation to follow.

The angels do not replace God. They intervene *because of*, not *in addition to*, God's vast and overwhelming presence to us, and for our sake. The presence of the angels is an intensification of His relationship with us, and reflects its beauty. They are the chosen means by which He will communicate with human beings, in such a way that we can stand before His light as well and not be annihilated.

God chooses to work through the ministry of angels to share His light with us. The angels, therefore, have a considerable task. This gives rise to the next consideration about the angelic world: How many angels are there?

Angels: An Uncountable Army of Light

The angels are created all at once in a divine act of creation. God creates them in such fullness that their very number is staggering to human perception. Sacred Scripture witnesses to the exceedingly great number of the multitude of angelic hosts. The prophet Ezekiel tells us that the angels are so numerous that their very movement makes an incredible sound: "Then I heard the sound of their wings, like the roaring of mighty waters, like the voice of the Almighty. When they moved, the sound of the tumult was like the din of an army" (Ez 1:24). Bildad, the Old Testament friend of Job, says that the angelic armies of God can't be counted (see Jb 25:3). The author of the Book of Deuteronomy says that as innumerable are human beings in all the nations throughout all of history, so too are the angels: "[God] set up the boundaries of the peoples after the number of the divine beings" (Dt 32:8; see Acts 17:26). The prophet Daniel describes the overflowing quantity of angels in God's presence: "Thousands upon thousands were ministering to him, and myriads upon myriads stood before him" (Dn 7:10; see Rv 9:16).

No one, throughout all of Scripture, can get a head count of the angels. The prophet Joel says, "The LORD raises his voice at the head of his army; How immense is his host! How numerous those who carry out his command!" (Jl 2:11). The author of the Letter to the Hebrews tells us that the angels are "countless" (Heb 12:22). The Letter of Jude expresses a similar belief to describe the Lord coming with all His hosts (Jude 1:14), as does the Book of Revelation (Rv 5:11).

The saints and theologians also lose count when it comes to angels. St. Dionysius explains that the blessed number of the armies of angels far surpasses and overwhelms our human numbering system.[11] St. Thomas Aquinas tells us that angels exist "in exceedingly great number, far beyond material multitude."[12] The medieval commentator Thomas Gallus explains that only a heavenly numbering system can count the angels.[13]

God alone knows the number of the hosts of angels.[14] God creates the angels in such great number for at least two reasons. First, the mystery of the Triune God is so overwhelming, it is only fitting that a multitude of angelic hosts serve to reflect the brilliance of the light of the divine glory. Second, because the beauty of the visible world that God creates in His plan is so profound, especially human beings created in His image and likeness, God will call on the angels in countless ways to make known the mystery of His divine providence. God permits the angels to assist human beings and all of creation to fulfill His designs.[15] To say that the angels, creatures of God, assist us in no way distances God from us. Rather, it conveys the specificity and closeness of His care. Tolkien writes that the angel is "not a thing interposed between God and the creature, but God's very attention itself, personalized. And I do not mean 'personified', by a mere figure of speech ... but a real (finite) person."[16] The angels are sent to serve "those who are to inherit salvation" (Heb 1:14). The brilliant light they reflect and their great number are not status symbols for the angels. Their brilliance and vast multitude reflect their calling and mission. Let us look more closely at this light-filled mission of the angels. The angels serve in inestimable ways through teaching and protection.

Their Light-filled Mission: The Angels Teach and Protect

St. Albert the Great explains the importance of light in the creation and work of the angels. St. Albert tells us that the light of God's glory shines on the angels in such a way that the angels then reflect and share that light with us, so that in the soul we see divine things.[17] The Book of Chronicles tells us that God sends His angels persistently (see 2 Chr 36:15). The angels intervene repeatedly, and these interventions are moments of supernatural light. St. Albert goes on to explain that there are two principal ways the angels intervene and reflect God's light to us.

First, the angels teach. For example, when the archangel Gabriel appears to Zechariah to announce the conception of St. John the Baptist, Gabriel teaches Zechariah (and us). In his announcement to Zechariah, Gabriel teaches how St. John the Baptist's place in God's plan follows upon the Old Testament revelation of salvation history (see Lk 1:16–17). Gabriel's announcement refers to the three classic sections of the Old Testament. Gabriel refers first to the Law: "And he will turn many of the children of Israel to the Lord their God"; Gabriel then refers to the prophets: "He will go before him in the spirit and power of Elijah"; and finally, Gabriel refers to the wisdom writings: "and the disobedient to the understanding of the righteous." As he teaches, Gabriel proclaims a summary of the Old Testament teaching as it will be fulfilled in St. John the Baptist in preparation for the Incarnation. Angels often teach when they appear. St. Paul also tells us that the angels delivered the Law: "it was promulgated by angels" (Gal 3:19). St. Stephen, the first martyr, attests that Israel received the Law through the testimony of angels (Acts 7:53). The very first verse of the Book of Revelation clearly explains that God made known all that is included in that book "by sending his angel to his servant John" (1:1). John then reported what he saw — the light of God's truth — through the work of the angel.

The Church's great theologians highlight the teaching role of the angels as well. St. Augustine teaches that the angels proclaim the Law with an "awesome" voice.[18] Alan of Lille, the twelfth-century French theologian known as the *Doctor Universalis* due to his widespread knowledge, explained how angels can reveal the beauty of God to us. Lille taught that a theophany (a visible manifestation of God to human beings) is the contemplative knowledge of angels revealed to human beings, which, when received as human knowledge, is known as theology.[19] The angels know and love God; they also know and love His creation. This combination of knowledge and love is what the angels illumine and announce when they teach.[20] In a poetic sense, we can say that the angels are camouflaged in light as they intercede, and teach us on God's behalf. They humbly blend into the action of God to convey His intervention to human beings. They can direct God's light to us so that we can receive it without being overwhelmed. Their concealment is not meant to make them hard to see, or for them to evade detection, but to highlight the action of God. It is this supernatural light of the action of God that they reflect in their mission and ministry.

St. Bernard of Clairvaux confirms the subtle action of the angels, and explains that they are God's agents who convey divine visions to men and women.[21] St. Dionysius agrees and tells us that the light of revelation of the things of God reaches human beings through the ministry of angels.[22] The *Catechism of the Catholic Church* teaches, "As purely *spiritual* creatures angels have intelligence and will: they are personal and immortal creatures, surpassing in perfection all visible creatures, as the splendor of their glory bears witness" (330). The angels take their ministry as teachers very personally.

This affection of the angels as teachers is personal for us as well. Even as we sit in a classroom learning theology, listen to a homily in Church, or do spiritual reading at home, it is the angels who minister deep in our intellect, attempting to free us from obstacles to belief and understanding of the ways of God.

In addition to teaching us, a second way the angels intervene is by delivering us from danger. The Patriarch Jacob, after praising God for His faithfulness, next speaks of "the angel who has delivered me from all harm" (Gn 48:16). The angel of the Lord intervenes when King Nebuchadnezzar has the young men thrown into the fiery furnace: "But the angel of the LORD went down into the furnace with Azariah and his companions, drove the fiery flames out of the furnace, and made the inside of the furnace as though a dew-laden breeze were blowing through it. The fire in no way touched them or caused them pain or harm" (Dn 3:49–50).

The theologians also describe the angels as defenders. Origen says, "How profound a mystery is the apportioning of souls to the Angels destined for their guardians! It is a divine secret, part of the universal economy centered in the Man-God."[23] St. Basil tells us that "an angel is put in charge of every believer, provided we do not drive him out by sin. He guards the soul like an army."[24] St. Justin affirms that God has "committed the care of men and of all things under heaven to angels whom he appointed over them."[25] They guard us especially from temptation, and they protect us for salvation.

The angels are closer to us than is the natural light around us. Supernatural light pervades every mission of the angels. It filled the mission of the angel who tamed the savage lions with the prophet Daniel (see Dn 6:23), the angel who instructed the priest Zechariah in the Temple (Lk 1:11), and the angel who appeared to the shepherds near Bethlehem (Lk 2:9). And supernatural light fills yet another mission that the angels had. In fact, this mission took place long before angels closed the mouths of the lions or made known the great prophecies. It was their earliest mission, the first mission to which God summoned the invisible good angels: to assist Him with the creation of the visible universe.

The Angels of Creation
Created first by God, the angels existed with Him before anything else in the visible universe. The angels existed before planets or oceans, animals or people. There was a time when it was just the angels and God. In His providence, God uses the angels as invisible instruments and ministers in His creation. God allows the good angels to serve as intermediate causes to assist Him in implementing His wise and loving plan. They do this with creation itself. The author of the Letter to the Hebrews says that "what is visible came into being through the invisible" (Heb 11:3). The original Greek translates more specifically, "What is seen was not made out of things which are visible." Of course, God does not need the angels in order to create the world. He needs nothing else outside of himself to create. God is the sole Creator of the world. He is eternal, and He creates all that exists outside of himself, including the angels, *ex nihilo* — out of nothing. Creation is an act of His complete and all-sufficient generosity. But God has so willed to allow His angels to serve as His instruments and ministers in creating the visible world.[26]

St. Irenaeus explains that God is like the architect of creation.[27] The angels administrate the beauty of creation as God creates the world. The angels are the first "day" of creation, and the other "days" of creation are the various glances of the angels around creation.[28] We can reread the account of creation, and as we hear God speaking, we see the beauty of each "day" illuminated through the intimate glance of the angels, these primary witnesses of creation, as they behold God's creation in Genesis 1:6, 9, and 11): "Let there be a dome in the middle of the waters, to separate one body of water from the other"; "Let the water under the sky be gathered into a single basin, so that the dry land may appear"; "Let the earth bring forth vegetation: every kind of plant that bears seed and every kind of fruit tree on earth that bears fruit with its seed in it."

Bouyer and Balthasar agree that God deliberated with the angels when He said, "Let us make human beings in our image" (Gn 1:26).[29] From this moment on, the good angels are spiritual companions, assisting human beings to see and understand the path to God.

Angels as the First Scientists

Due to their closeness to God and their ordering of the beauty of creation, the angels know created things as more than mere facts. They study and love creation deeply, because it comes forth from God. It is out of this love that the angels know every aspect of creation intimately and thoroughly.

According to St. John Cassian, as they see all the visible creatures God created proceed forth from nothingness, the angels cry out with loud voices in admiration and praise of the Creator.[30] The prophet Isaiah tells us that the Seraphim, the highest order of angels, after they speak of the Lord's holiness, immediately speak of how it fills the creation and the earth: "I saw the Lord seated on a high and lofty throne, with the train of his garment filling the temple. Seraphim were stationed above; each of them had six wings: with two they covered their faces, with two they covered their feet, and with two they hovered. One cried out to the other: 'Holy, holy, holy is the LORD of hosts! All the earth is filled with his glory!'" (Is 6:1–3).

God charges the angels with the continual care and administration of creation. The angels work in the here and now so that the carrying out of God's plan may reach its fullness. They ceaselessly patrol the earth to intercede for peace in the world and comfort among nations (Zec 1:8–17; 2:2–5). The psalmist says of the angels: "Their span extends through all the earth" (Ps 19:4, Breviary). St. John refers to one of the powers of the angels over the visible universe: "After this I saw four angels standing at the four corners of the earth, holding back the four winds of the earth so that no wind could blow on land or sea or against any tree" (Rv 7:1).

Origen tells us, "There are angels in charge of everything, of earth, water, air and fire: all the elements alike. They are also used by the Logos as instruments to regulate the movements of the animals, the plants, the stars and even the heavens."[31] St. Augustine agrees and says, "Every visible thing in this world has an angelic power placed over it."[32]

Origen says that the angels help guide creation as an ordered whole: "The ministries of earth, the many departments of nature, are allotted to the heavenly Virtues; fountains and rivers, winds and forests, plants, living creatures of land and sea, whose various functions harmonize together, by the Angels directing them all to a common end."[33]

St. Gregory the Great concurs: "In this visible world nothing takes place without the agency of the invisible creature."[34] St. Thomas Aquinas, too, emphasizes that the angels guide and administer corporeal creation.[35] The theologian Jean Daniélou says that the Christian "believes that mysterious beings rule over fountains and forests, watch over families and cities, protect the young child, and lead them to paradise." The angels are "countless protective presences."[36] In this sense, the angels take part in God's governance of the natural and physical world, carried out in a way proper to themselves.[37] But the good angels do not lord their knowledge of creation over us.

Through their understanding of creation, the angels can reflect, reveal, and particularize the light of God's glory to human beings in the most specific of circumstances. They help us to follow God more deeply as we grasp His mysteries "understood and perceived in what he has made" (Rom 1:20). St. Umiltà of Faenza tells us, "God gave them [the angels] knowledge of every science with which they might be servants and ministers of divine greatness."[38] An angel's intellect is so far superior to ours and "possesses such penetration, that he is able, at one glance, to take in the whole field of science lying open to his perception, just as we, at a glance, can take in the entire field of vision lying exposed to our eyes."[39] Since God gave the angels knowledge of every science, and the angels make use of this knowledge as they engage with the visible world, the angels are, in effect, the first scientists. The angels know the entire created world with instantaneous precision in a direct spiritual way, in a single stroke, even material things.[40] Fr. Walter Farrell points out that "the angels are naturally masters of the visible world."[41] When we study creation and probe the mystery of existence, we always first engage with the angels, even without knowing we are doing so. The angels then guide us into the intelligibility of everything and every science — from medicine to music; from architecture to law; from social science to biology, to business, to communication; from linguistics to industry, to accounting; from sound to psychology, and, especially, theology. Angels mediate teaching through bringing the beauty of all of God's designs to light.

The angels work within the physical, natural world to carry out God's purposes and convey His plan to us.[42] They administrate creation in such a way that, in the world, God's "invisible attributes" are clearly seen (see Rom 1:20). The angels also see that God created human beings in His image and likeness (Gn 1:26–27), and that it is their task to make known to human beings the saving mysteries of Christ (Heb 1:14). The angels are "down to earth" for our sake.

That's a wonderful gift from God. But someone else has noticed the beauty of creation. Someone else has taken note that human beings are created in the image and likeness of God. Another angel has taken note of the saving mysteries of Christ, and the great humility of God. That angel's name is Lucifer. He has beheld the astounding beauty of creation, the marvel of the sciences. And his response, and that of the angels who side with him, is "down to earth" in a far different way from that of the good and holy angels.

PART II

THE FALLEN ANGELS:
Rejecting the Light

Chapter Four

LUCIFER AND THE FALLEN ANGELS: UNLIMITED FURY

A n important question arises in catechetical classes. The question is a signal. It means that the students are drilling down, reasoning well, and making connections between theology and the real world. The question is this: "Why did God create evil? Why did He create the devil and the evil angels?"

The short answer is that God did not create anything evil. Scripture is quite clear that all that God creates is good, including the entire heavenly host of angels (see Gn 1:4, 31). As we have seen, God creates the entire heavenly host of angels when he says, "Let there be light" (Gn 1:3).

But the very next verse of Genesis takes us further into the angelic world: "God saw that the light was good. God then separated the light from the darkness" (1:4). We often take this verse to refer to the twenty-four-hour daily division of night and day. But this verse doesn't refer to that separation. The separation of the natural lights came on the fourth day of creation. The separation of light and darkness on the first day refers to a separation of far greater depth and significance. The separation of light and darkness is the permanent separation from the good angels, who choose holiness, from the fallen, disobedient angels who, though created good, freely choose sin, evil, and darkness. Notice that though God did say that the creation of light "was good," He does not say that the separation of light from the darkness "was good." This is because that separation arises from the choice of some angels to permanently choose evil.

The deeper explanation of the origin of evil begins here and takes us down a seldom traveled, but crucial, theological path. To explore it, we need some background information on several matters: the creation of all the angels in "initial beatitude," the nature of the angelic intellect, the choice of the angels, and the fall of Lucifer. Understanding these seldom-explored topics will shed light on how sin works with human beings, and the true nature of the battle in which the good angels assist and guard us.

Angels: Busy in Initial Beatitude

Let's look first at what's called "initial beatitude." Angels are not robots. God did not program them like computers. He created them in goodness, and with free will. Though they were created good, they were not *immediately* permanently confirmed in goodness.[1] The goodness in which all the angels were created was a period of initial beatitude. This period was different from "supernatural beatitude," or the Beatific Vision.

It was initial, but not in the sense of "partial." The angels in this moment of initial beatitude were not lacking in any knowledge of the mysteries of God. Initial beatitude was the moment after the angels were created, but before the creation of the visible world itself, in which they immediately received the revelation of the knowledge of the mysteries.[2] The angels had all the perfection of their nature, and in this perfection God gave them the vision of His resplendent goodness in such a way that they were filled with all of the knowledge, insight, and awareness that they needed to make a free choice to serve God. As they engaged in this moment of initial beatitude, the angels shared and participated in the divine life, and enjoyed resplendent gifts of nature and grace. They were divinely perfected with supernatural virtues and graces, such that they could merit, after undergoing this period of probation in initial beatitude, the reward of eternal happiness.[3] In this period of probation, their knowledge was free of any defect, and so comprehensive that they could choose good or evil — to merit eternity with God, or to lose Him and the life of heaven for all eternity. They received the superabundant light of grace to know God's glory and to freely respond to His invitation to love Him. They were called to freely respond based on what they saw in initial beatitude. All they had to do was turn to God in one free act to secure supernatural beatitude.

Now to the second matter, that of the angelic intellect. St. Augustine comments on the advanced intellect of the angels, explaining that they "have no need to look up to this [creation] and to read so as to know [God's] word. They 'ever see [God's] face' (Mt 18:10) and there, without syllables requiring time to pronounce, they read what your eternal will intends. They read, they choose, they love. They ever read, and what they read never passes away."[4] The angelic intellect is far superior to the human intellect. You and I come to know things gradually, through a process of prolonged learning by means of our physical senses, which takes place with a lot of consecutive effort over many years. Because they are pure spirits (not composed of matter), angels do not need such development to come to know things. They are fully aware of their knowledge from the beginning of their existence. Angels need nothing repeated, and they do not forget what they know. Their angelic intellect knows creation through and through. Boudon explains:

> They [the angels] possess wonderful intelligence; what
> the greatest geniuses have not been able to comprehend,
> is perfectly understood by them. They know many
> things in one and the same moment, and without the
> least difficulty. Their manner of understanding is not
> like ours; at the first sight which they have of a thing,
> they know its whole import and all its consequences —
> hence they are called by excellence "Intelligences."[5]

St. Paul tells us that the mysteries of God are hidden from us
— "the mystery hidden from ages and from generations" (Col
1:26) — but He allows the angels to grasp much more directly
the mysteries of Christ. In grasping these mysteries, the angels
also understood that the mysteries they encountered in initial
beatitude would unfold in time, and be proclaimed especially in
the Gospels. The angels grasp the light of these mysteries in a
most excellent way. St. Faustina says, "Because of their profound
knowledge of God, no person on earth, even though a great saint,
has such knowledge of God as an Angel has."[6] Pope St. John Paul
II agrees, and notes that the intellect of a pure spirit has a knowledge of God that incomparably surpasses in perfection human
knowledge.[7] John Paul explains that the angels can see into the
depths of God's greatness. The sensational genius of the angels
allows them to be fully occupied in an entirely contemplative
and completely active engagement of the mysteries of God.

This is why the angelic intellect is so important for the question of evil. In initial beatitude, the angels explored the mysteries
of God in such a way that they required no additional or further
clarifying information in order to decisively choose to permanently embrace or reject God. Because of their nature as intellectual creatures, they understand all at once. They do not need to
"remake" choices based on further information, as humans do.

In the first moment of initial beatitude in their creation, the angels had all the information they needed to make a free choice to love or reject God. Unlike the angels, we human beings are not created in initial beatitude. We learn over time. Our intellect is also not as clear or immediate as that of the angels.[8] We have erasers on the top of our pencils, so to speak, and can remake our bad choices. The angels cannot.

As a result, original sin has different consequences for us than the sin of the fallen angels does for them.[9] We exist in time and, until we leave time at the moment of death, can remake our decision for or against God. The angels' choice for or against God that they made in initial beatitude was made with decisiveness and determination, based on complete and superior knowledge that their choice was final and irreversible.[10] The evil angels cannot regret their bad choices, and cannot repent of the evil they do.

The Incarnation: The Center of Angelic World

What the angels know is of great importance here. Of all the mysteries the angels learned in initial beatitude, one mystery stands out: The angels learned that the Word would become flesh and dwell among us (see Jn 1:14). They understood that the Son of God was to be sent by the Father into the world for human beings and for their salvation. St. Paul proclaims that the Son of God, "manifested in the flesh," was "seen by angels" (1 Tm 3:16).

In this, the angels saw the bewildering humility of God — that the Second Person of the Blessed Trinity, without ceasing to be true God, would humble himself to be born of a Virgin for the salvation of human beings. The angels learned the mystery of the Incarnation — that the Son of God would, as the Letter to the Hebrews says, "'for a little while' [be] made 'lower than the angels'" (Heb 2:9) — that the Second Person of the Blessed Trinity would take flesh and assume human nature. St. Clare of Assisi writes to St. Agnes of Prague, and recounts how the angels are enthralled by the humility of the Incarnation, that its beauty "eternally awes the blessed hosts of heaven."[11]

The angels also learned the role they would play in this: The archangel Gabriel would one day proclaim the Incarnation at the Annunciation to Our Lady (see Lk 1:30–33); an angel would one day proclaim the Incarnation by an annunciation to St. Joseph in the depths of a dream (Mt 1:20–21); and one day, the angels would announce it to the shepherds in Bethlehem (Lk 2:10–12).

In learning of the mystery of the Word made flesh, the angels further probe the mystery of the extreme humility of the Son of God. The good angels are fascinated by the humility of God. In creating human beings, God humbly includes, because of the nature of love itself, the possibility that those He loves the most may freely reject Him.[12] God does not use power to control those He loves. The good and holy angels never grow bored before the unfathomable humility of God. The good angels are ever more fascinated by the humility of God, and long to make it known to human beings.

Why does the mystery of the Incarnation fascinate the angels? Because it is so fundamental to their mission. Every action they ever perform proceeds from and returns to the Incarnation. They learned in initial beatitude that all the mysteries of Christ connect to the Incarnation. They also understood the implications these mysteries hold for human beings and for the angels themselves.

The angels understood that God would create human beings in His own image and likeness: "Let us make human beings in our image, after our likeness" (Gn 1:26). As they beheld the mystery of the Incarnation, the angels also immediately comprehended God's tremendous love for human beings, that they would be the adopted sons and daughters of God. In the beauty of the Incarnation, the angels realized that the omnipotent Creator of the universe, who needs nothing else, nonetheless creates and longs to be in relationship with human beings. As the psalmist says, "He raises the needy from the dust, lifts the poor from the ash heap, Seats them with princes, the princes of the people" (Ps 113:7-8). It is as if the angels are speaking in Psalm 8:

> What is man that you are mindful of him,
>> and a son of man that you care for him?
> Yet you have made him little less than a god,
>> crowned him with glory and honor.
> You have given him rule over the works of your hands,
>> put all things at his feet:
> All sheep and oxen,
>> even the beasts of the field,
> The birds of the air, the fish of the sea,
>> and whatever swims the paths of the seas.
>> (Psalm 8:5–9)

In knowing this, the angels also knew that God intended to give human beings a share in His own dominion over the created universe: Human beings would "have dominion over the fish of the sea, the birds of the air, the tame animals, all the wild animals, and all the creatures that crawl on the earth" (Gn 1:26). The angels first saw the order of creation, from mineral, to vegetative life, to the animals, then second, human beings in special relationship to God. Third, they saw *contrast* between themselves and human beings.

In initial beatitude, the angels also learned something about themselves. They are called to love the Son of God, and therefore they are called to love those He loves: human beings. The author of the Letter to the Hebrews captures this point: "For to which of the angels did God ever say: 'You are my son; this day I have begotten you'? Or again: 'I will be a father to him, and he shall be a son to me'?" (Heb 1:5), and "Surely He did not help angels" (Heb 2:16). St.

Thomas explains the implication that by the gift of grace, human beings can merit to be equal to angels.[13] The Book of Revelation assures that Christ is so close to the human beings who cling to Him that He will even testify before the angels on their behalf: "[I] will acknowledge his name in the presence of my Father and of his angels" (Rv 3:5). The angels are, as the author of the Letter to the Hebrews writes, "ministering spirits sent to serve, for the sake of those who are to inherit salvation" (Heb 1:14; see CCC 331). Boudon says that it is "the highest ambition" of the holy angels "to share their thrones with us."[14]

This means that the angels encountered this light of the glory of the Lord in initial beatitude as the messengers who were preparing to be *sent* to proclaim those mysteries, and make the light of those mysteries known to human beings. St. Paul also tells us to seek out these mysteries (see Col 3:1–2), and the angels help us to do just that. The key task and message of every angel is to reveal to human beings "the inscrutable riches of Christ" and make known "the mystery hidden from ages past in God" (Eph 3:8–9). Drawn deeply into the mystery of God's love in initial beatitude, the good angels yearn to participate ever more deeply, so deeply that St. Peter speaks of the "things into which angels longed to look" (1 Pt 1:12).

Knowing all this, the angels had to choose. The Book of Job recalls the joy the angels expressed at the first dawn of creation in initial beatitude, "while the morning stars sang together and all the sons of God shouted for joy" (Jb 38:7). After learning (instantly, remember) the mysteries of the Son of God with their advanced intellect, each of the angels then made a single, free decision to accept or reject God. This decision took the form of an act of charity, or love, for God. With this decision, they confirmed themselves permanently in the goodness in which they were created — or outside of it, as we shall see.[15]

The angels who made this free choice to love God then

moved from initial beatitude to permanent beatitude. They forever joined themselves to God.[16] Joined eternally with God, the holy angels continually sing out with joy at the mystery of God's love for human beings and the mystery of the Incarnation.

And yet, within the jubilant chorus, a discordant note is heard. And here we come upon the answer to the question asked in catechism class: Where does evil come from?

Lucifer: Bearer of Light

Among the heavenly chorus, in initial beatitude, there was one angel of note. His name was Lucifer. His name means "Bearer of Light." St. Gregory the Great tells us that Lucifer, before his fall, surpassed the hosts of angels in brightness, and was the most distinguished among them.[17] In fact, St. Thomas tells us that God had placed Lucifer in charge of the terrestrial order of the world.[18]

As were all the angels, Lucifer was summoned to make the first act of charity by which he would forever attain final beatitude, the eternal vision of God.[19] Lucifer refused. He rebelled. Whereas the good angels responded to initial beatitude with delighted humility, Lucifer, along with some of the other angels whom he led, chose a different course.

Like the other angels in initial beatitude, Lucifer contemplated the truth that the Son of God, the Second Person of the Blessed Trinity, would take human flesh in the Incarnation. He saw the tremendous depths of the humility of God, by which He would create human beings in His image and likeness (see Gn 1:26), and the tender love with which He would love human beings, each one unique, irreplaceable, and unrepeatable. Lucifer also saw that God would allow man and woman to be co-creators with Him through marriage and human procreation. He saw that God would even go so far as to allow man to eat manna, the "food of angels" (Wis 16:20).

Finally, Lucifer understood that the truth of the Incarnation would lead to yet another resplendent truth: As Pope St. Leo the

Great says, "Man's nature would rise above the ranks of angels and archangels."[20] On the basis of the cascading mystery of God's love for human beings, the angels also intuit the consequent truth of the world to come: "For it was not to angels that he subjected the world to come, of which we are speaking" (Heb 2:5). It is on this same basis that St. Paul says, "Do you not know that we will judge angels?" (1 Cor 6:3). In initial beatitude, among all the truths that Lucifer saw, he saw that God would become man and elevate man to the supernatural order.[21]

Lucifer would not accept that human beings, creatures of body and soul, would share his standing and judge him, a pure spirit. He would not accept the mystery of the Incarnation, nor its attendant mysteries. He realized that, in the Incarnation, God the Son would unite to himself, not angelic nature, but human nature — a nature far beneath that of the angels. The Incarnation horrified him and the angels who sided with him. The Incarnation, and every truth connected with it, he and the evil angels saw as an unspeakable humiliation because of their pride, by which they had become absorbed in the beauty of their own nature.[22] Lucifer did not make the act of charity by which he could have made beatitude permanently his own.

Lucifer's Anti-Confession: *Non Serviam*

Instead, Lucifer said to God, "*Non serviam*" — "I will not serve" (see Jer 2:20). In doing so, Lucifer completely refused his mission to announce and serve the mysteries of the Incarnation of the Son of God. Lucifer, who should have cast unfathomable light on the mystery of the divine humility, now seethes and brims with malice. He, who was so wondrously raised up by God's grace, now turns his gaze away permanently from the light of God's glory in utter contempt for God. He chooses to oppose God, to fight Him with all his might, with all the powers of his angelic nature. He descends defiantly into self-centered pride. Turned in on himself, Lucifer clenches his own hideous, resistant, and discordant will.[23]

Lucifer was not created evil. God created him good. Lucifer became a devil — evil, through his own decision. He willfully permanently rejected the beatitude in which he was created.[24] Lucifer, a created though supernatural being, permanently became an outright enemy of God, who in serious and sinister wickedness now seeks to rebel against God continuously. Lucifer is also our enemy. He attacks human beings because we remind him of his fall from grace.[25]

Where does evil come from? The answer is that Lucifer's rebellion is the beginning of evil. St. Cyril of Jerusalem gives us the concise answer: "The chief author of sin, then, is the devil, the author of all evil. ... After being created good he became a devil of his own free choice."[26] Parente further explains: "All of the wickedness and the resultant suffering, misery and death in this world can be traced back to Satan."[27] The Lord Jesus says that the devil "does not stand in truth, because there is no truth in him" (Jn 8:44).

The devil not only rejects the light; he attacks it. By his act of disobedience Lucifer attempts to wreak havoc against the providence of God and to set himself as the beginning and goal of all that exists. God answers the prophet Habakkuk and, speaking ultimately of Lucifer, says, "Terrible and dreadful is he, from himself derive his law and his majesty" (Hab 1:7, NAB). This spurs some of the other angels, now known as the evil angels, to give their free consent to his rebellion as well.[28] The Book of Revelation refers to Lucifer as the dragon and the stars as angels when it says, "[The dragon's] tail swept a third of the stars out of the sky and flung them to the earth" (Rev. 12:4). St. Thomas affirms that this verse is the basis for attesting that Lucifer's sin is the inducement of the sin of the other rebellious angels who sinned with him.[29] These are the demons — the fallen angels, created supernatural beings who were meant to love God, but who now oppose Him. St. Matthew refers to the devil's angels (see Mt 25:41), and St. Paul speaks of "the spirits of wickedness" (Eph 6:12, Douay-Rheims).[30] The demons are Satan's strange allies and, as we shall shortly see, our terrible adversaries. People ask, "How many angels fell with Lucifer? How many demons are there?" Relying on the Book of Revelation, we believe that one-third of the angels fell. The Book of Revelation refers to Lucifer as the "dragon," and the fallen angels as "stars" when it says, "[The dragon's] tail swept a third of the stars out of the sky and flung them to the earth" (Rv 12:4, NIV).

Lucifer Cast Down

The Book of Job tells us that God immediately saw the evil choice Lucifer and the angels who followed him had made: "In His angels He found wickedness" (Jb 4:18, Douay-Rheims, see also 15:15). Genesis tells us that after Lucifer's definitive choice against God, there was then a separation, of which we spoke earlier: "God saw that the light was good. God then separated the light from the darkness" (Gn 1:4). The separation is the fall of Lucifer and the angels who rebelled with him.

Because of his sin, Lucifer was cast down from heaven. The reverberation is felt throughout Scripture. The Book of Judges alludes to the fight between the good and evil angels: "From the heavens the stars fought" (Jgs 5:20).[31] The psalmist likewise says, "Behold the man! He did not take God as his refuge, but he trusted in the abundance of his wealth, and grew powerful through his wickedness" (Ps 52:9).

Cassian tells us that the prophet Isaiah, in a chilling passage of prophetic vision, describes the pride of Satan and his fall in vivid detail:

How you are fallen from heaven,
 O Morning Star,[32] son of the dawn!
How you have been cut down to the earth,
 you who conquered nations!
In your heart you said:
 "I will scale the heavens;
Above the stars of God
 I will set up my throne;
I will take my seat on the Mount of Assembly,
 on the heights of Zaphon.
I will ascend above the tops of the clouds;
 I will be like the Most High!"
No! Down to Sheol you will be brought
 to the depths of the pit!
      (Isaiah 14:12-15; see Ezekiel 28:1–10)

Notice how Isaiah calls attention to Lucifer's diverse and detailed knowledge of creation. Lucifer knows creation so well because of the precision of angelic knowledge. It was that exalted knowledge, which he plumbed in original beatitude, that Lucifer then used wrongly by pridefully refusing to obey God. The words of Isaiah capture the nature of Lucifer's pride: "Your wisdom and your knowledge led you astray, And you said in your heart, 'I, and no one else!'" (Is 47:10).

St. Augustine, Origen, and St. John Cassian tell us that a passage from the prophet Ezekiel recounts Lucifer's fall.[33] Notice in the passage Ezekiel's description of Lucifer's exalted position in initial beatitude prior to his sin. It begins: "You were a seal of perfection, full of wisdom, perfect in beauty. In Eden, the garden of God, you lived; precious stones of every kind were your covering." [34]

After describing his beauty and importance, the passage continues: "Your commerce was full of lawlessness, and you sinned.

Therefore I banished you from the mountain of God. ... Your heart had grown haughty because of your beauty; You corrupted your wisdom because of your splendor." The rest of the passage describes God's turning him to ashes: "You have become a horror, never to be again" (Ez 28:16, 17, 19).

The prophet Daniel refers to Lucifer's fall in his account of the King of Persia,[35] and to Michael as the great prince who assists in the battle (see Dn 10:13; 12:1). The prophet Jeremiah recounts Lucifer's fall as well: "The destroyer of nations has set out, has left its place, To turn your land into a desolation, your cities into an uninhabited waste" (Jer 4:7).

The reverberation of the fall of Lucifer continues in the New Testament. St. Jude speaks of "the angels too, who did not keep to their own domain but deserted their proper dwelling" (Jude 1:6). St. John tells us that "the devil has sinned from the beginning" (1 Jn 3:8, see also 5:18).[36] St. Paul confirms that Lucifer was cast down from heaven because of the sin of pride, and he warns believers not to "be puffed up with conceit and fall into the condemnation of the devil" (1 Tm 3:6, RSV2CE). St. Peter confirms: "God did not spare the angels when they sinned, but condemned them to the chains of Tartarus" (2 Pt 2:4).

The Lord himself testifies that hell was created "for the devil and his angels" (Mt 25:41). The Book of Revelation tells us further that "a loud voice" is then heard in heaven: "For the accuser of our brothers is cast out, who accuses them before our God day and night" (Rv 12:10). It describes Lucifer as "a star that had fallen from the sky to the earth. It was given the key for the passage to the abyss" (Rv 9:1–2).

In one of the most startling passages in all of Scripture, the Book of Revelation depicts the scene of Lucifer's horrific disobedience:

> Then war broke out in heaven; Michael and his angels bat-
> tled against the dragon. The dragon and its angels fought

back, but they did not prevail and there was no longer any place for them in heaven. The huge dragon, the ancient serpent, who is called the Devil and Satan, who deceived the whole world, was thrown down to earth, and its angels were thrown down with it. (Revelation 12:7–9)

The archangel Michael contends with Lucifer and says, "The Lord rebuke you" (Jude 1:9, RSV2CE), as Lucifer is cast out.

The Three Temptations of Our Lord

Another passage in Scripture teaches us about Satan's fall. We do not often associate it with his fall, but seeing it in that light may help us to more deeply internalize how vital the work of the Lord is in defeating Satan. Recall that immediately after His baptism by St. John the Baptist, the Lord is driven into the wilderness where he fasts for forty days and forty nights (see Mt 4:1–2). Satan then puts three temptations to the Lord (Mt 4:3–11). It is often said that this passage shows Our Lord conquering the temptations of gluttony, pride, and greed.

We often associate the temptation in the wilderness with the preparation for the public ministry of the Lord and His solidarity with us in temptation. That is true enough. We do learn from Christ in this account how to respond to temptation. But something even deeper is at work in the passage. The temptation in the wilderness is where the devil, for the first time, faces and attacks the Incarnation directly, "seeking to compromise [Jesus'] filial attitude toward God" (CCC 538). The three temptations are an echo of Lucifer's rejection of the truths he learned in initial beatitude. Let's examine how this takes place.

In the first temptation, Satan tempts the Lord to turn stones into bread (see Mt 4:3). On one level, this is a temptation to the sin of gluttony. But it's deeper than that. More is at work in this temptation than simply the temptation of the Lord to alleviate

his physical hunger. Even when Satan tempts our senses to gluttony, lust, or greed, he's always first attacking the intellect. He
wants to fool us into finding our worth in some luxury, all the
while really telling us that we are worthless and no good. Why
does he do this? Remember that in initial beatitude, he saw the
beauty of creation. He fell because he believed that all of creation
should center on him and be his possession, not the Lord's gift —
that he, Satan, should be able to control and manipulate creation
to serve him, rather than he serve it. This temptation is about
something deeper: It reiterates Satan's original selfishness that all
that exists, even stone and bread, should be subject to him. And
if stone and bread should be subject to him, all the more should
human beings. Because he can't control existence, he wants to
ruin it not only for the human beings God loves, but for the Son
of God himself.

Jesus knows what Satan is really saying. He reminds Satan of
the original sacred truth of creation itself, which Satan learned in
original beatitude: That every creature — even angels — lives not
by the power to manipulate and control creation, to use it for his
own desires, "but by every word that comes forth from the mouth
of God" (Mt 4:4). Jesus affirms that the order and use of creation
can in no way be separated from the purpose with which God has
directed it, and in that order human beings have a special place
which even the angels serve and cannot manipulate in disordered
ways.

In the second temptation, Satan takes the Lord to the Holy
City and to the pinnacle of the Temple (see Mt 4:5). From that
height, Satan tempts the Lord to throw himself down. He says,
"For it is written: 'He will command his angels concerning you'
and 'with their hands they will support you, lest you dash your
foot against a stone'" (Mt 4:6).

On one level, this temptation appears to be about enticing the
Lord to make trivial use of the divine power: to make Him take

pride in His power, by using it to show off.

But, again, it's deeper than that. We can hear behind Satan's words an echo of his original rage against that truth he learned in initial beatitude: That he as an angel is sent to serve the Incarnation, to convey this mystery to human beings, creatures God will elevate, even above him. In this second temptation, Satan mocks the Lord. It is as if he is contemptuously saying, "How dare you create angels in all their magnificence to serve and guard mere human beings!" Again, Jesus knows what Satan is really saying. The Lord's response is simple: "Again it is written, 'You shall not put the Lord, your God, to the test'" (Mt 4:7). The Lord reminds Satan of the heavenly truth that the Lord is God ... and Satan is not, a truth he hates.

In the third temptation, Satan shows the Lord all the kingdoms of the world and promises them to the Lord if He will worship him (see Mt 4:8–9). This third temptation appears at first to be about greed. Imagine the wealth of all the kingdoms of the world. Put together every fortune made on Wall Street, the bank accounts of every robber baron, the treasure rooms of every kingdom, and the riches of every government. The combined worth of all these riches, jewels, and treasures is staggering. But on a deeper level, this temptation recalls Satan's disobedience, for which he was cast out of heaven. In his pride, Satan had attempted to overthrow the providence of God by setting himself above Him. In this third temptation, Satan does it again. It's not about the money and the greed — it is about what is behind the money and the greed. Greed is the follow through of pride. Satan wants the Son of God to worship him. That is why Lucifer was cast out of heaven. And the Lord responds in this temptation with the same penal sentence as Lucifer received previously: "Get away, Satan! It is written: 'The Lord, your God, shall you worship and him alone shall you serve'" (Mt 4:10). Satan is again cast down, just as he was in his original disobedience in heaven. The good angels then come and minister to the Lord (Mt 4:11). Just as Satan replayed his heavenly rebellion in the temptation in the desert, so too the good angels reiterate their original choice of permanent beatitude and come and minister to Christ. Jesus' resisting temptation is not just a model for us. It's a promise. As the *Catechism* teaches, "Jesus' victory over the tempter in the desert anticipates victory at the Passion, the supreme act of obedience of his filial love for the Father" (539).

Lucifer's Permanent Sin

Lucifer's sin is all the more distressing because the angels are not prone to sin.[37] It was fully in Lucifer's power not to sin. He did not have to sin. He and the angels who sinned with him were not fated to sin or predestined to sin. Lucifer and the angels who fell with him made one, fully informed, eternally determinative choice to reject God definitively and "irrevocably" (CCC 392). It is important to note that Lucifer does not simply "slip into" the sin of pride. The fallen angels did not sin out of weakness or ignorance. There was no further information they could have received to help them see their error. Lucifer and the rebel angels committed the sin of angelic pride and did so in the face of their deep knowledge of God's holiness.

Prior to his fall, Lucifer dwelt close to God, and it was within this very closeness, his supernatural elevation, that Lucifer's animosity and motivation for his sin arose.[38] Lucifer commits his sin of angelic pride, and does so in the supernatural order. Lucifer's pride arises in full force based on his superior knowledge. The sin of pride, committed in the supernatural order by an angel, has malevolent consequences. This is why his sin is so terrible: He sinned directly out of the strength of his angelic resemblance to God. St. Jerome tells us that God had set His own impression on the first of the angels, but that Lucifer destroyed this resemblance completely and irrevocably in his sin.[39] Lucifer's angelic being, in his one, fully informed, determinative choice of disobedience against God, fully conformed Lucifer irrevocably to pride. He has concentrated his entire being in his choice. Therefore, by this choice, Lucifer rejects God "radically and irrevocably," and, at the same time, attempts to exalt himself above God (CCC 392).

The permanence of the devil's sin does not reflect any defect whatsoever in the infinite mercy of God (CCC 393). Nor is it a harsh penalty simply doled out by God. Lucifer and the evil angels made a fully deliberate choice out of raging hatred for God, for which they never have any regret or repentance whatsoever. They have resolved once and for all to be the hostile enemies of God. The choice is permanent and eternal. They remain obstinate in the malice forever: as the psalmist says, "The uproar of your adversaries ... goes up continually" (Ps 74:23, NRSV). Lucifer and the evil angels become absorbed in themselves, such that they entirely derange their own nature permanently with pride.[40] Lucifer forever desires to be exalted, praised, and honored above anything else in the universe. Pride blinds. The devil's pride is so blind that he can never recognize his own defeat. Venerable Bede explains, "Those who refuse to be humble cannot be saved."[41] The Book of Tobit says, "In pride there is ruin" (Tb 4:13, NRSV). Lucifer and the evil angels' aversion for God and all that God has created will never end.[42]

Lucifer is so completely a creature of pride that he does not see his being cast down from heaven as a defeat. He sees it as a victory. Cast down, the devil thinks he is winning. This is the nature of pride. It interprets everything that happens to it as victory, even what is really defeat. And since he sees himself as winning, the devil has no remorse. He only attacks all the more.

Lucifer's Envy of Human Beings

Pride leads to envy. That explains why Lucifer and the evil angels work incessantly against the human beings God loves. Lucifer's malicious pride against God gives rise to his monstrous envy of human beings. As we've seen, the devil sees that man, created from the dust of the ground, is called to a glory similar to that which Lucifer himself once had. We have what he expects for himself. He cannot bear that the Son of God would empty himself (see Phil 2:6–8), be obedient, and humbly deign to be conceived of a Virgin, born in a forgotten, unnoticed stable, and be a servant — to convey the light of that glory to human beings.

Lucifer did not want to *convey* the light. He wanted to be the light. Since he cannot be the light, he seeks to attack God by destroying those whom God loves: human beings. He attempts to destroy them through sin and death. Every human sin has its ultimate source in the dreadful sin of Lucifer. We can now understand better the devil's attack on humanity and the Church, beginning with original sin.[43]

Chapter Five

LUCIFER'S ATTACK
ON HUMANITY

We can see now why it is important that we not regard the devil as a fairy-tale figure, little more than a Halloween character, or only a troublesome disrupter who trips us up from time to time. The *Catechism* teaches that "evil is not an abstraction, but refers to a person, Satan, the Evil One, the angel who opposes God" (2851).[1] We can see from his rebellion and fall that he is far worse than a mere symbol for evil or an abstraction. We ought not to have a neurotic or obsessive, exaggerated fear of the devil, fixating on him as if he were around every corner.[2] But we should have a prudent fear of him and the fallen angels. In one sense, we do not fear him enough (see Mt 10:28).

The prophet Habakkuk says of the devil and the evil angels: "They are terrifying and dreadful ... They scoff at kings, ridicule princes; They laugh at any fortress, heap up an earthen ramp, and conquer it. Then they sweep through like the wind and vanish— they make their own strength their god!" (Hab 1:7, 10–11). Even St. Paul was attacked by the devil, as he tells the Thessalonians:

"For we wanted to come to you—certainly, I, Paul, did, again and again—but Satan blocked our way" (1 Thes 2:18, NIV; see Rom 1:13, 15:22). The devil is a fallen angel, literally hell-bent on our destruction. The devil and his fallen angels are personal beings with intellect and will, capable of focused and determined activity. Prudent fear of the devil and the fallen angels leads us not to paralyzing anxiety, but to take deeper refuge in Christ, especially through the sacraments.

Like the devil, the evil angels also seek to destroy. The psalmist is speaking of the demons when he says, "They scoff and spout their malice; from on high they utter threats" (Ps 73:8). The psalmist reminds us frequently that the evil angels plot against human beings: "The wicked prowl on every side" (Ps 12:8, NKJV); "they intend evil against you, devising plots" (Ps 21:12). "The wicked plot against the righteous and gnash their teeth at them" (Ps 37:12); they "practice deceit, [their] tongue plots destruction; it is like a sharpened razor" (Ps 52:2, NIV) by which they commit slander (Ps 119:23).

We must not forget that Lucifer, in his devilish pride, saw the Incarnation as an insult. Why does Lucifer hate the Incarnation so much? St. John explains it well: "Indeed, the Son of God was revealed to destroy the works of the devil" (1 Jn 3:8; CCC 394). In all that Christ does, He is conquering Satan. Lucifer is therefore the enemy of the Annunciation — the moment when the angel Gabriel announced to Our Lady that she would be the mother of God's only Son. Some Church Fathers, Daniélou tells us, believed that "the sin of the angels was refusing to accept the Incarnation of the Word, because it raised mankind above them, which they found humiliating."[3] He emphasizes that "throughout an entire tradition the sin of the angels was explained as their refusal to recognize the dignity of Adam created in the image of God."[4] The Dominican scholar Father Farrell agrees, "The devil's pride led him to object to God uniting imself personally with human nature, which would have diminished his own glory as an angel."[5] The French poet Paul Claudel tells us that when Lucifer heard the merciful plan of redemption, he turned against God.[6] The devil envies us because God deigned to take our nature, not that of angels, in the Incarnation. When the devil sees human beings, he finds again the beginning and circumstance of his fall.

Lucifer hates the Annunciation to Our Lady, since with her "Fiat" the Son of God became incarnate in her immaculate womb (see Lk 1:38). Lucifer always remains the enemy of the Incarnation, of God come in the flesh. St. John, in his second letter, emphasizes the point: "Many deceivers have gone out into the world, those who do not acknowledge Jesus Christ as coming in the flesh; such is the deceitful one and the antichrist" (2 Jn 1:7).

But Lucifer also saw the Incarnation as God's fatal flaw. And he believed he could exploit and use this flaw to thwart the providence of God. Even now, he supposes that, cast down from heaven, he is better positioned to be the enemy of God and to destroy God's plan. The devil believes he can ruin God by destroying human beings, especially through sin. And so, not only does evil wage war against God; the devil and the evil angels "set themselves against us [human beings] too. They prepare trouble and strife for us."[7] After he was cast down, Lucifer unleashed on earth the malevolent war he began in heaven — a war that continues to this day.

The psalmist says of the devil and his angels, "Their plan is only to destroy" (Ps 62:5, NAB, 1970). They plan to destroy us through death, to return us to the dust from which we came, and they tempt us to sin so as to lead us to death. Death is the devil's solution, his attempt at eternal revenge. God did not make death. The Book of Wisdom makes the connection: "For God formed us to be imperishable; the image of his own nature he made us.

But by the envy of the devil, death entered the world" (Wis 2:23–24).[8] The devil tempts us so that we will sin and choose spiritual death.

This is the nature of temptation: The devil wants to smuggle the things of the world into our souls so that there is no room anymore for God. "Whether he is aware of it or not," Balthasar warns, "the sinner who deliberately leaves the area between himself and God in which God's Holy Spirit operates — communicating divine grace and a divine mission to him — enters a contrary realm inhabited by a spirit that is hostile to God."[9] Temptation is very dangerous. The devil must therefore design and disguise his temptations to make sin look like we are having the time of our life. He does this with meticulous intensity.

Temptation's Wardrobe: Disguise

As feverish and sinister as Lucifer's designs of destruction are, the early part of temptation would never win an Academy Award. Hollywood would find the first act of a real-life temptation downright boring. Temptation's first moves are always meant to appear as little more than a ripple, as imperceptible as it is crucial to the devil's overall plan. The devil puts a lot of work into temptation because he knows its far-reaching consequences. He never wants us to notice him, so he rarely approaches us directly. He prefers to approach us under a disguise. And he's good at disguises. St. Paul warns us that the devil can disguise himself even to appear "as an angel of light" (2 Cor 11:14).

Cassian also points out the subtlety of the devil's disguised attacks. The devil's goal, like the snake's, is to afflict us with his poison before we even see him.[10] Cassian urges us to be on guard against Satan "as a dangerous enemy," who attempts to injure us "by a deceptive show of friendship."[11] The devil wants us to think he poses no threat and, if possible, to see him as an ally and even a friend. Balthasar emphasizes that "evil necessarily veils and misconstrues itself" so as to throw us off its trail.[12] St. John Chrysostom warns that even though the devil cannot create power, he can make us think he has it.[13] The evil angels are beings of power who manifest themselves in power and seek dominion.[14] The devil wants to influence human beings by spiritual means, to sift us (see Lk 22:31). He even resorts to physical measures (see Lk 13:11; Mt 12:22; Rom 8:35; and Rv 2:10) to tempt and persecute us.

Why does the devil disguise himself? Why wouldn't he just attack us directly? You would think that the devil would intervene directly, right away — as soon as he sees someone decide to make a new start, go to confession for the first time in years, consider a vocation, or go to Mass together as a family. Why wouldn't the devil overtly interfere in a terrifying apparition or troubling nightmare the very day a husband and wife decide to go to Bible Study together or start saying a family Rosary? The devil disguises himself for at least three main reasons.

First, because Satan's goal is to induce us to use our will against God. In temptation, he does not "make" us do anything. If the devil were to overpower us directly, it would be *he* using our will to reject God, not *us*. The whole point of his work is that he wants *us* to reject God. Though he can incite us to thought by kindling the passions, the devil still wants to appear blameless, to come off at first as inexperienced — a lightweight, an amateur. The devil's ultimate goal is for us to sin and freely reject God's love on our own, not with his directly forcing us by an outward display of his threatening presence; he wants to set us up to misuse our freedom, so that we step firmly into the sinkhole already cracking open around us with his every word.

He needs a disguise for a second reason: He does not want us to notice him as he approaches, because the devil obviously intervening would drive most people directly to confession and Mass. His pride is so furious that we would see it immediately if he approached us directly. His evil is so ugly, divisive, and hideous that he must disguise it to make it appear useful and good so we will desire it. He wants to look ordinary, with nothing distinctive about him, fading into the background so we don't detect his presence. In tempting us to sin, he wants to proceed in shades of gradually intensifying darkness, remaining undetected for as long as he can.

It's the way he's worked since the beginning. "Even as in the Garden of Paradise with our first parents," Fr. Lyonnet emphasizes, "Satan carefully conceals his designs, and is most careful at first not to reveal the slightest malicious intention."[15] The devil tries to duck below our radar. "At first we almost fail to recognize him, he insinuates himself unobtrusively, slyly, calling no attention to himself. Only towards the end does he throw off the mask, permitting us to catch a glimpse of his hatred and ill will," Fr. Féret writes.[16]

That's why St. Paul urges us to be vigilant, "so that we might not be taken advantage of by Satan, for we are not unaware of his purposes" (2 Cor 2:11). St. Teresa of Ávila emphasizes this point: "It is very necessary we don't grow careless in recognizing the wiles of the devil. ... He enters little by little and until he's done the harm we don't recognize him."[17] Fr. Lyonnet also warns that behind all the tricks the devil uses, more is at work: "Behind this sensuality, this love of the flesh and of the world, there is hidden a 'power that is eminently intelligent, a true person.'"[18] With his angelic intelligence he conjures up disguises so he can have more access and leverage in our lives as he sets traps for us. The psalmist warns us: "As I go along this path, they have hidden a trap for me" (Ps 142:4). St. Paul prays that we "escape from the trap of the devil, who has taken [us] captive to do his will" (2 Tm 2:26, NIV).

A sign of advancement in the spiritual life is that the attacks of evil grow more prominent.[19] As the believer advances in the spiritual life, the devil relies less on disguises. The sign that one is growing in the spiritual life is not necessarily long periods of un-interrupted mystical prayer, continuous pious thoughts, or feeling like life is all working out. It can be quite the opposite. It is when he sees us sticking with the Christian commitment over time and growing close to Christ through thick and thin, come what may, that the devil begins to attack more directly.

The devil is very frightened when he sees a Christian being faithful and able to endure, even in the tedious ups and downs of life. He gets very disturbed when he sees that we no longer compulsively measure our worth by good feelings, or that our faithfulness is not based on "getting something out of" our religion. It is then that he attacks us more directly. And it is here that we arrive at a crucial point in the spiritual life. As Bouyer writes, "The crucial point" in the spiritual life is "the necessary struggle against the demon."[20]

The third reason the devil disguises himself when he tempts us is simple: With a disguise, he thinks himself safe from counterattack.[21] He doesn't want his fingerprints at the scene of the crime. He wants us to attribute our difficulties and sins not to evil, but to a flaw in our personality, family history, or just mistakes we have made. He knows he can't keep his hideousness hidden very long, and if we saw it, we would be much more ready to flee to Christ for refuge. The devil wants us to see the things he offers us in temptation — greed, lust, anger, envy, etc. — simply as the way of the world, as the way things really work. As such, he wants us to see faith as a childish myth, so that even when the wicked tail of these worldly "pleasures" eventually starts to strike us with its repeated cruel backlash, we will have nowhere to turn. And so, the devil disguises his approach so that we will not be alarmed and flee to the Lord for rescue; and if we do eventually become alarmed, we will feel ourselves cornered and stuck.

The Devil's Approach to Beginners: *Attract* Rather Than *Attack*

But what about the beginner in the spiritual life? Fr. Bouyer tells us that the devil does not directly approach the beginner in the spiritual life. Rather than *directly attack* the beginner, he prefers to *indirectly attract* the beginner in the spiritual life, to detour him or her away from God. "The devil first reveals himself indirectly, under his usual masks of the world and the flesh."[22] His masks are carefully shaped to appear as everything we ever wanted in our lives.

Recall the parable that Jesus told concerning the weeds among the wheat (see Mt 13:24–30, 36–43). The weeds are a poisonous Palestinian weed called darnel. It looks like wheat until it has grown,[23] so if it is sowed in among wheat, one must wait until both are grown to tell them apart. This is the devil's ruse when he tempts the beginner. In the early stages, he seeks to imitate goodness, and so attract us. In its early stages, temptation never appears ugly.

Our Lord warns us of this subtlety. Recall the parable of the man building a house (see Lk 6:48). The house may be built on sand or on solid rock. The house is the image of the dwelling of God in the soul. God wants to build His grace-filled dwelling within us. Jesus tells us in the parable that whether the house is built on sand or on rock, the torrent still assaults it. The "torrent" stands for temptation. We are tempted, whether we build our spiritual life on rock or on sand. It is interesting to note that the Greek for "torrent" is *potamos*. This comes from two words, *pinō* and *potos*, which, when put together, mean "to receive the things of the world into the soul." In temptation, the things of the world assault the soul like a torrent. But we don't always see the destructive force of the torrent, because at first, the devil makes the things of the world look attractive. The things of this world are the riches we seek.

Riches do not have to be a big bank account or a fancy sports car. The "riches" of this world are anything we want too much, but don't have. They can be as simple as the attention on which we insist from someone else, reputation, or getting our own way in the smallest things.

Here's one way this works: The devil induces us into brooding over little things for a long time. He points out how life is not working out for us, how people are not seeing things our way, how everything seems a struggle. He often then suggests that we also ruminate on how everyone else — from the commuters next to us on the expressway, to the checkout person at the supermarket, to our neighbors — seems to have it all together: They get the promotions, and we are left behind. They join the big firm, and we don't get an interview. They have so much money, and we live paycheck to paycheck. The devil wants us to blame each other, and not him. He gets us all fueled up with thinking about what we lack, and then spurs us on to chase it with the most uncharitable methods.

The devil's temptation is to make us think we deserve our riches, and he tempts us to get them on this world's terms: force, trickery, deceit, revenge, blame, politics, manipulation. This is one of his most clandestine (and effective) disguises. The Desert Fathers referred to the snares that the devil suggests to our thinking as *logismos*. The *logismos*, the theologian Fr. Simon Tugwell explains, is a "train of thought which engages the mind, so that bit by bit one drifts away from what one is supposed to be doing into a world of fantasy."[24] St. Thomas Aquinas tells us that the devil acts on the human imagination, the human mind, and the human senses.[25] The devil instigates and incites thoughts by the desire for what we think of, by enflaming the passions and moving the imagination.[26]

And knowing our behavior and fears, the devil deepens our fears with lies that he wants to become part of our inner thinking. St. Paul was referring to this inner false thinking when he said, "But I am afraid that, as the serpent deceived Eve by his cunning, your thoughts may be corrupted from a sincere [and pure] commitment to Christ" (2 Cor 11:3).

These thoughts are like pollen in the spring season — you don't see them until you begin to feel the itchiness or the first throbs of the headache. You have not consented to the temptation or the thoughts yet, but already you experience a certain level of discord.

It is important for us to know that the devil's power is not infinite; he cannot directly act on our intellect or will.[27] Though they can make suggestions to us, St. Thomas notes that the evil angels cannot place thoughts in our minds.[28] God alone knows the heart (see Jer 17:10). The angels do not know the secrets of our hearts.[29] Even on Holy Thursday evening, when the Gospel tells us that "The devil had already induced Judas, son of Simon the Iscariot, to hand [Jesus] over" (Jn 13:2), the meaning is that the devil had "thrown" or "scattered" the suggestion at Judas, but the devil could not override Judas's freewill. Judas had to freely consent to the suggestion of the evil one for the devil to gain a foothold in him. The devil cannot force us to do things. His assaults are strong, because he's so subtle. He creeps up on us and acts at the periphery of our imagination, memories, and thoughts. We don't notice he's influencing us unless we're on the lookout.

The angels are invisible to us, but we are not invisible to them. We might even say that the angels see right through us. They can discern our motives and intuitions, our reasoning and intentions.[30] The devil uses his angelic intellect to read our vulnerabilities, our fears, and our wants, and lie to us based on our fears. He operates with expert acumen about human behavior. He can surmise better than any psychologist about the nature of our thoughts by our external behavior. And from our words and actions, he can reason back to the nature of our thoughts and desires, from which our words and deeds arise.[31]

The devil can therefore deduce our individual aptitudes, our particular history, and our personal vulnerabilities.[32] He does not know us in the interior depths of our soul or in the thoughts of our heart, but he knows us through what he has seen us do.[33] He gains insight into what is in our heart by watching the patterns, tendencies, and behaviors of our daily life. He uses this knowledge to plant a seed of misunderstanding that, unaddressed, grows up into a grudge. He looks early in our lives for any little crack, any small misunderstanding, and there he wedges in his crowbar of separation, attempting to pry us away from the unity of love into the seclusion of the self. To do so, he suggests things to us. St. Teresa of Ávila noted that the devil brings certain thoughts to mind: thoughts of the world, of esteem, and of the self.[34] The devil will twist any circumstance, as incidental as it may be, to suggest division: someone not holding a door for us (They really don't like you — in fact, not many do ...); two colleagues closing the door to the office as we pass by (They are talking about you, how you dropped the ball on that project ...); or a busy friend is delayed returning our call (Aren't you getting the message? They don't like you. If they liked you, your phone would ring ...).

The devil knows us the way a doctor deduces the condition of our lungs by listening to our breathing, and our state of health by learning our family history, our diet and exercise routine, and our test results. It's all data he puts together to get an amazingly intimate and accurate view of our strengths, and especially our weaknesses.

Yet the devil cannot force a thought or desire on us that we do not want to have. This is why he must rely on disguises and lies to make his temptations attractive. He customizes his lies to fit our personal experiences and circumstances.

Temptation: Spiritual Hypothermia

The most common mistake we make about temptation is that we often think it takes place in a mere moment — a flare-up of passion that overwhelms us, or that we manage to resist and we quickly get over. We may think that the moment of temptation is when we see the expensive car and wish we had it; when we sit at the computer and are tempted to gamble or to look at porn; or when we want to yell at our spouse. But these are only the "punch lines" of temptation. The devil's first move in temptation is not with glitz. By the time the devil is giving the punch line, he has been building the temptation up for several hours, or days, or months, or even years — until it doesn't feel like a temptation at all, but the normal thing to do.

Temptation functions a lot like hypothermia. The devil wants to freeze our soul, to make it devoid of the warmth of grace and the excitement for virtue. If we don't learn to recognize temptation from the beginning, the devil's ways (the ways of the world) begin to numb us. But, as with hypothermia, we do not know we're growing colder. In fact, as with hypothermia, we think we are growing warmer: *I don't really have to go to Sunday Mass when I am on vacation. God knows where I am in my heart. Why not just sleep in? I usually go to Mass the rest of the year. Everyone needs a break … Why not look at the porn site? After all, it's not like I am out with a prostitute. I'll only look for fifteen minutes. That'll be an improvement over last time … Why not gossip? Everybody does it.* At some point, hypothermia begins to feel good. The things the devil tempts us to do feel good. They feel right.

Temptation is meant to make the wicked threat of sin appear beautiful, as something we cannot do without. The devil wants to blend in, to make his suggestions appear ordinary and for our benefit. Temptation takes the form of thoughts that seem to fit in and make sense at first, but they carry a type of slow-acting poison with them. He wants to spark in us a habitual way of thinking that sabotages our way of viewing everyday life. The thoughts present an apparent way for handling a situation, for moving ahead, or for working through a dilemma. The devil uses the ways of the world as the raw material from which he makes his darts. Cassian reminds us though, that the devil is a lurking enemy who seeks to put something into our hearts.[35]

As the theologian Heinrich Schlier wrote, every temptation spreads "a deceptive semblance over reality, surrounding it with an aura of deceit; this he may accomplish by conjuring up deliberate and calculated illusions."[36] The devil has influence in the world. The Book of Revelation tells us that the devil "was thrown down to earth, and its angels were thrown down with it" (Rv 12:9). Jesus referred to the devil as both the "ruler" and the "prince" of this world (see Jn 12:31; 14:30; 16:11, NIV). St. Paul called the devil "the god of this age" (2 Cor 4:4; see 1 Jn 5:19). Paul reminds us that our struggle is against the power of the spiritual forces of evil (Eph 6:12). The devil seeks to exercise his considerable influence in the world and on us by his lies and illusions. In enacting this influence, he does not principally aim his illusions at the abstract. He seeks to take hold of concrete circumstances in our life, and distort them with his illusions and lies as he goes "to and fro" on the earth. He seeks to influence the world and us, mainly through temptation. The devil's goal throughout temptation is to pull us from one temptation to the next, so that we stumble farther into the old illusion he spins faster and faster. He strings along his temptations to seem sophisticated, but they are spiritual frostbite.

Genesis 3: An Ancient Warning

The spiritual hypothermia of temptation is revealed especially in the first temptation in all of history: that of Adam and Eve in the Garden of Eden (see Gn 3). As Fr. Lyonnet explains: This chapter, "without giving [the devil's] name, without instructing us concerning his nature, without explaining his origin, nevertheless teaches us practically all that we know about the Devil."[37] The *Catechism of the Catholic Church* points out: "Behind the disobedient choice of our first parents lurks a seductive voice, opposed to God, which makes them fall into death out of envy. Scripture and the Church's Tradition see in this being a fallen angel, called 'Satan' or the 'devil'" (391).

As we reflect on Genesis 3 in detail, we discern the concrete way in which the devil approaches all of us in temptation. For example, the first verse tells us a lot about what we need to know about temptation: "Now the snake was the most cunning of all the wild animals that the LORD God had made."

It is a sobering admonition. It occurs before the devil even utters a syllable of temptation: *"Now the snake was the most cunning of all the wild animals that the LORD God had made"* (3:1). This is a crucial point. When we are tempted, we are not on a level playing field. The devil is "more crafty" than any other wild animal God had made. To say that the devil is "more crafty" is not simply saying that he is a con man; he is far more than a con man, and is far worse. This verse is a warning to us: Lucifer and the fallen angels, even after their fall from heaven, retain the power of the superior angelic intellect.[38] Their disastrous choice, by which they permanently rejected God, does not undo their creation as angels. They're evil angels, but they still have their angelic powers, including the genius power of the angelic intellect. Their fall makes them evil angels, but they retain the power of the angelic intellect itself. They turn that angelic intellect now to serve purposes dense with darkness and thick with evil. The evil angels remain spiritual, personal beings, yet rather than using their intellects' power to reveal the mysteries of God, the unholy angels turn their angelic intellect against human beings and the entire created world. St. Dionysius reminds us that "the angelic gifts bestowed on them have never been changed inherently, that in fact they are brilliantly complete."[39] St. Thomas Aquinas says, "[The evil angels] abuse their nature for evil."[40] Cardinal Daniélou agrees and observes that the fallen angels "still have a semblance of power until the judgment day."[41]

We see the devil's craftiness in the very first temptation. Before he says anything else in Eden, the devil asks, "Did God really say ... ?" The devil admits the existence of God. More than that, he takes the existence of God for granted. And, strikingly, the devil also admits that God reveals himself and speaks to human beings.

Most people believe in God. It's a lot easier for the devil to corrupt that belief than to eliminate it. So in Genesis, he does not suggest that the woman is silly for believing in God, or tell her it's time she grew up and thought for herself. You would think the devil would want to recruit people to atheism, to deny the existence of God. But the devil's goal is not atheism. In fact, the devil has little time for atheism; he prefers *indifference* to atheism. This is one of his masks: The devil does not want us to deny the *existence* of God; he wants us to deny *God*. Satan wants us to admit that God exists, believe in God, and then to reject and turn away from God with our will.

To accomplish his ends, however, the devil benefits far more if we do not believe in his, the devil's, existence. Satan wants to put the focus on God and take it off himself. He likes to propose that it would be silly to believe that he, the devil, exists. To conjure this disguise, he simply has to whisper, *"Do you really believe in a personal evil being? That is so medieval. This is the age of technology, depth psychology, and jet travel. Evil is just a combination of bad genes, bad parenting, and bad luck. You're not really going to believe that behind every evil there is an intelligent, unseen being plotting sinister demise? You'll be the laughingstock of the neighborhood, the academy, the work place. Come on now! It's not even Halloween."* As Pope St. John Paul II said, "It is in [the devil's] 'interest' to make himself unknown."[42]

If we do admit the effects of evil in the world, the devil would like us to think that evil is just a nameless social malaise over society. St. Paul reiterates the stakes we are up against, undoubtedly from his own experience in contending with the evil one: "For our struggle is not with flesh and blood but with the principalities, with the powers, with the world rulers of this present darkness, with the evil spirits in the heavens" (Eph 6:12, see also 2:2). The original Greek phrase for "the heavenly places" is *ta epouranios*, and is better translated as "high places." It is not a reference to the heaven where God is, but the invisible forces that drive the material world.[43] The evil angels retain their vast, cutting-edge knowledge, perception, and comprehension of all the human sciences. They possess all possible natural expertise in knowing the biological world, of animals and all the elements.

The devil would like us to forget the fact of his advanced intellect. Satan and his angels use all their angelic power to incorporate layers of disguise, lies, and deception into one temptation after another. As Lucifer, the devil knows the created world well. He remains familiar with all the treasures of the world. He knows the price of gold better than any brokerage house. He can spot the flawless diamonds, sapphires, and emeralds. There is no ounce of silver ore to which he does not know the way. He has had a hand in drafting every treasure map. He knows the stock market better than all the Wall Street analysts combined.

Satan, who as Lucifer was in charge of the beauty of the material universe, can now make use of the powers of the physical world for his evil purposes. He does not control the physical world, but he can seek to influence it through his angelic power. Recall his words to Our Lord when he showed Him all the kingdoms of the world: "I shall give to you all this power and their glory; for it has been handed over to me, and I may give it to whomever I wish" (Lk 4:6). What does this mean for us? It means that "the goods of this world can only be had on the terms of the prince of this world," as Tugwell notes.[44] The psalmist knew well the old trick of riches and greed. In greed, riches continually consume the mind: worry about not having enough, fear of losing what one does have, and the continual drive to get more and more and more.[45] And yet, the riches themselves amount to nothing, "a mere breath the riches [man] hoards, not knowing who will have them" (Ps 39:7, Breviary). Recall the question Our Lord poses in the parable of the rich fool to the man who greedily hoards money, and whose life is required of him that very night: "The things you have prepared, to whom will they belong?" (Lk 12:20). As Herman Hendrickx has pointed out, "It is clear to whom that piled up wealth will ultimately go."[46]

Notice one thing, though. How long did Satan show the Lord all those kingdoms of the world? For only "a single instant" (Lk 4:5). That is all the time the grand illusions of the devil can last — if we refuse to entertain them. When seen through the lens of humility, the devil's lies dissipate in the moment of their casting. The devil would like us to think him absent, all the while preferring us to think that if he does exist, he has long since retired or simply given up. But that is far from the case. His fury is as fresh today as it was in the moment of his fall from heaven. And we see it in his terrible lies, which he seeks to disguise … at least at first.

Chapter Six

THE COILING ENEMY: THE FIVE SHINY DISGUISES OF PRIDE

The devil is "a liar and the father of lies" (Jn 8:44). The lie is always the "favorite weapon in his arsenal,"[1] because the only way to disguise evil and make it appear attractive and good is to lie; thus, the lie is always Satan's counter-strategy to God's loving plan.[2] Every temptation we face from the devil is a slow maturation of a lie that's been carefully crafted to make good appear evil, and evil appear good. All sin begins with a lie that is disguised as a promise. Recall the temptation in the Garden of Eden: "But the snake said to the woman: 'You certainly will not die! God knows well that when you eat of it your eyes will be opened and you will be like gods, who know good and evil.'" (Gn 3:4–5). There is a lie hiding in plain sight in the serpent's words: "You will be like gods." He got Adam and Eve thinking that they lacked something, when in fact they already had it. They already were like God. The lie is in that the devil used the future tense. The account of creation tells us that God said, "Let us make human beings in our image, after our likeness" (Gn 1:26).

St. Teresa of Ávila says, "Anything the devil gives is like himself; a total lie."[3] And one lie leads to the next. The devil wants his lies to linger in our thoughts. He wants us to get used to lies so that they become our way of life, and we never question them. The devil uses subtle lies to introduce turbulence into our daily life, and then he keeps reminding us of those lies. He wants to brand our souls with the marks of sin so that our very conscience is consumed. This is what sin does in the soul. But without the subtle groundwork of deception, the rest of the temptation would collapse.

The devil and his fallen angels are deeply cunning, able to weave intricate lies to ensnare us. The devil is the serpent — "the coiling enemy"[4] — whose lies form an intricate web of coils to ensnare us. Temptation is not so much like the devil coaxing us to cross a line into sin as it is his luring us to step into his coils, which he has arranged to twist and tighten around us. The prophet Isaiah refers to the serpent as the "coiled serpent" (Is 27:1). The coils are a form of twisted, crooked distortion by which he seeks to surround us in our discernment so as to draw us off course. His coils entwine us first and foremost in our thinking, leading us into bitterness and hostility that form chains around our soul. Over time, without our noticing, we find ourselves trapped and entwined tight in coiled habits of a thorny circuitry of sin, and we hardly know how we got there.

There are many bands to Satan's coil, but we will look at five principal ones in this chapter: 1) isolation; 2) the mirror; 3) undue concern for the opinions of others; 4) gossip; and 5) the occult.

Isolation: The Devil's Favorite Game

One of the devil's first deceptions is the lie that we are alone. He proposes isolation — division from others — as the answer to everything that is bothering us and the way to get ahead. He advises isolation as the next step for whatever we face. Isolation is the "outer band" of what will soon grow into the hurricane storm of temptation; it is poison disguised to look like the cure. The devil waters our isolation with impatience to make it grow, delighted when we get annoyed, tighten up, and lash out. The devil loves isolation because he can tempt us more easily when we are alone, cut off from others.

One way the devil isolates us is through worldly success. He can never get enough of our worldly success, or our isolation. The devil sprinkles his suggestions like little frantic darts he throws at us in and through the daily, ordinary moments of life. When we are frustrated with a situation at work that did not go our way, the devil suggests, *Why not just do it on your own? You show them, just turn your back and do your own thing.* The devil leads us down a busy trail of frantic activity to impress others, to say the smart thing or the witty comment — and to do it all while looking composed and professional. He urgently, endlessly prods us to try to "figure it (life/work/relationships) out," and when we cannot, he blames us. All the while, he is wrapping us up in a tense perfectionism, so that our quest can never really be satisfied. He wants us to be obsessed with what we lack — which is usually exactly what others seem to have. The devil wants us fixated on what we think is "wrong" with ourselves, with others, or just with life in general.

He constantly leans over our shoulder to suggest to us that we should be the smartest person on the project at work, the strongest person in the contest, or the most popular or respected person in the room. And when others do not treat us as the smartest, the strongest, or the most popular, he stokes our feelings of rejection and resentment. Or it may be a problem in our past, the way we were raised, or our finances. Whatever the content, the devil wants us fixated on what we think is wrong so he can stir disappointment into pride.

Isolation is pride's most common disguise. Pride does not begin with someone claiming the place of honor; it begins long before that, and it grows best in isolation because those who are isolated easily become self-preoccupied. Pride also discourages true self-knowledge (humility). In the distortion of pride, we don't see the real impact our sins have on other people. If we don't see our sinful impact on others, then we never have to confront our sins and faults. The pull of pride is strong and constant, and when we keep ourselves isolated from others, pride can find its way in without us ever appearing overly conceited.

The devil also wants to ensure that our isolation deepens. In our society, he does this by encouraging us to take refuge in our electronic devices. While technology provides many benefits, it can be like a coil that tightens around us and deepens our isolation, as we turn to screens as a means of escape, rather than facing the complexities of real life. We look to computers and smart phones as substitutes for relationships, rather than as aids to real relationships with others. If life isn't "clicking" for us, the screen certainly will, and the screen can easily become a lifestyle. Our devices flood us with information all day long. It is as if we are seeking intimacy with information to replace friendship and real connection. Screens are a portal to exhaustion and isolation, even as they pretend to bring us up-to-date.[5] Then, when we turn back to the real world — to class, work, friends, family — it all seems more difficult, because our screens do not train us for real relationships, but for superficial ones. The screen is designed to isolate us in an unreal world.[6] How can we avoid this subtle trap of the devil? Look for the fruits: impatience and anger are key signs that we are spending too much time with a screen. If we get impatient when a file takes too long to download, or angry when the Wi-Fi does not work properly, or the printer jams again, this is a sign that we have far too much of ourselves invested in the one-way world of the screen.

Ultimately, every temptation to isolate us is rooted in this lie: *You are worthless. And, by the way, you're the only one who is worthless — your friends, your coworkers, even your enemies; they have it all together. What happened to you?* If the devil can succeed in isolating us, he's much more likely to be able to get us on a false path, so that he can ultimately destroy us.

The Mirror: The Devil's Favorite Toy

The devil's game of isolation leads us to keep bumping into his favorite toy: the mirror. There are few places where lies thrive like they do in front of a mirror. Think about physical mirrors, like the one you probably have in your bathroom. Just as there are physical mirrors that reflect our physical appearance, we also "carry around" spiritual mirrors as we go through our day. Every temptation is like the devil lifting a mirror in front of us as he whispers in our ear, "How do you look?" He wants us to be obsessed with how we appear, how we sound, how we look to others. No data point is too small for our inspection in this spiritual mirror. *How do my kids look? How does the front of my house look? How am I coming off in this meeting?*

Spiritual mirrors are when we look at and overthink everything we do: from what we say, to what we look like, to trying to figure out what others think of us. Interestingly, every mirror contains something of a lie, because mirrors reflect in a distorted way.[7] When we're looking at our reflection, we're seeing it backwards. Mirrors get everything backwards. So when the devil raises a spiritual mirror in front of us, he's inviting us to look at a distorted version of ourselves — and to believe that it's real. Recall the first time the devil speaks in all of Scripture. He makes no grand and convincing statement against the existence of God, or persuasive argument as to why the evil way is the best way. Instead, he simply asks a question (and raises a spiritual mirror with it): "He asked the woman, 'Did God really say, "You shall not eat from any of the trees in the garden"?'" (Gn 3:1). He is not pushy or sinister or insistent. He does not appear to be threatening. On the contrary, when he begins the temptation, he makes no more fanfare than someone stopping to ask for directions. The devil is out to undo all of creation, but as a master of disguise, his approach appears to be a casual encounter — with a mirror attached. He suggests to Eve what she doesn't appear to have, and wants her to focus exclusively on that.

Most physical mirrors have frames. The same is true of the spiritual mirror the devil uses. As he holds up the mirror before us, he frames everything in terms of isolation: We are the only ones who are alone on a Friday night, whose families hold grudges, who feel awkward, who worry. He wants looking in his mirror to become our lifestyle, leading to comparison, idealization of others, and ultimately, false expectations for ourselves. Each morning, the devil puts that mirror up in front of us, suggesting that we obsess about this or that quality in ourselves. Each night, he harvests the events of our day and puts the most negative spin on them to influence our thinking.

St. Teresa of Ávila tells us that the devil assaults the soul with "heavy battery" in order to win it over.[8] He will "circle hell a thousand times," "attack us in a thousand ways," and generate "a thousand other obstacles" to lure us with his lies and "stir up tempests so as to do us harm."[9] He will even "wear himself out trying to lead the soul to perdition."[10] And all he needs is his mirror, which he wants to turn into a prison for us. He wants us to be trapped there in front of it, staring into the mirror of our own pride and ego. We fall into his trap when we gaze into his mirror, dragging it along with us throughout the day, making it the lens through which we view everything.

The question *How do I look?* tightens the coil of temptation further and sets the stage for the devil's favorite question: *What do they think of me?*

The Devil's Favorite Question
The devil continually poses a question for each of us: *What do*

others think of me? From board rooms high atop Manhattan, to classrooms in the heartland, to lines at the grocery store around the world, that question is asked countless times a minute in a thousand different ways. The question does not appear evil in itself, and it can even seem to be a reference point for prudence. In reality, though, this question fuels worldly fear. The more we strive to please others and be who we think they want us to be, the more we lose touch with who we really are and who God calls us to be.

We do not always ask this question consciously. In fact, the devil would prefer we always have it unconsciously in the back of our minds. He wants us to be constantly striving to do the impossible: to intuit from people's facial expressions, words, or body language what they think of us. And we respond to his prodding, attempting innumerable times a day to decipher what others think about us. We scan for the smallest hints, parsing every word, gesture, or glance for signs of approval or rejection. This hyper-vigilance stirs up anxiety, becoming a subtle way of life that exhausts us. It can also lead us to show off, as we seek to impress others with our own fireworks.

The devil wants us to ask: *What do others think of me?* not just now, in the moment, but during our entire life. He wants us to regret the past, dread the future, and fear the present. Then, as chaos rages, he suggests that we turn to sin to feel better: to steal to get what we deserve, to drink, to shop for things we don't need, to overeat, to act out sexually, or to be uncharitable to others to finally "show them."

Finally, as this question becomes part of our way of life, the devil suggests the answer: *You're a mistake. You don't really fit in. Others don't like you; they just put up with you.* The devil wants us to think what he believed from the beginning: that human beings are a mistake. It is important to remember that while we human beings do make mistakes, we are never a mistake. The belief that I am a mistake is shame. Mistakes can actually be valuable, if we allow them to teach us important lessons. Instead of letting mistakes be a lesson, we often turn them into shame. Shame is never a good thing. When we give in to shame, we internalize the belief that because we make mistakes, we are a mistake. Through his tools and toys of isolation, the mirror, and making us constantly worry what others think of us, the devil wants to wrap us up in shame. When we are enveloped in shame, we naturally shut God out. Once we are so absorbed in shame, we tend to hate ourselves (a good definition of the sin of pride). This is a deeper layer of the devil's coils of temptation, which he tightens and uses to draw us into lashing out at others. Once we hate ourselves enough, we turn that hatred outward. And one of the principal ways we lash out is through gossip.

Gossip: The Devil's Favorite Radio Station

Of all the natural elements of the world over which the devil has power, perhaps the most scary is his ability to influence and lead astray ordinary human language and conversation. The first time the devil speaks in all of Sacred Scripture, from all the resources at his disposal based on his angelic intellect, he chooses to introduce sin to human beings using gossip: "Did God really say not to eat of any tree of the garden?" With this question, Satan lures Eve into talking about God by suggesting that God has misled Adam and Eve.

Satan's ploy is literally the oldest trick in the book (appearing as it does in Genesis 3): Make a statement by asking a question. Far from naïve, the devil's question to Eve is a direct attack on God. The devil, though fallen, is an angel, which means he has an advanced angelic intellect,[11] so it's not as if he overheard God speaking to Adam and Eve and just wants clarification. Instead, while he seems to be quoting God, he's actually distorting God's words. God had said, "You are free to eat from any of the trees of the garden except the tree of knowledge of good and evil" (Gn 2:16–17). God gives man everything, "every tree that was delightful to look at and good for food" (Gn 2:9). Man's freedom is exceptionally wide: He may eat of any tree of the garden, except for one.

The devil's seemingly innocent question makes it sound as if God forbade them to eat of every tree in the garden. He makes the garden sound like a prison, not a gift. The devil also subtly inserts the adverb "really" to indicate a kind of incredulity, as if what God was asking is somehow strange and ludicrous; as if God is not only strict, but also out-of-touch. St. Francis de Sales reminds us that the devil believes that by criticizing God, the devil will increase his own worth.[12]

Then, the question hangs there. The temptation has begun. In suggesting that God has lied, it is the devil who lies. By simply adding the word *really*, the devil gives us the first terrible glimpse of his all-consuming pride: Satan pretends to be the authority — to double check, correct, and now belittle God. The devil, with one simple word of gossip, invites doubt and intensifies fear and worry.

At the same time, the devil flatters Eve by his question and tempts her to pride by suggesting that she, a mere creature, can parse and judge God's words. The devil's words always contain a charming venom. He always remains "the accuser of our brothers [who] is cast out, who accuses them before our God day and night" (Rv 12:10). And so, St. Paul wisely warns, "Avoid profane, idle talk, for such people will become more and more godless" (2 Tm 2:16). St. Paul also urges us to be vigilant so that "no one may deceive you by specious arguments" (Col 2:4).

Gossip began in the Garden of Eden, and it has continued since the Fall, throughout human history. Later in Scripture, we read about a plot against the prophet Jeremiah, which is founded on gossip and lies. His enemies contrive a plot against Jeremiah, saying, "Let us destroy him by his own tongue. Let us pay careful attention to his every word" (Jer 18:18). The psalmist also knows the sting of gossip: "They slandered me without ceasing; without respect they mocked me, gnashed their teeth against me" (Ps 35:15–16). Gossip does not know lesser degrees; thus Jeremiah's "every" word is noted, and the assault against the psalmist is "without ceasing." In the Gospel, gossip plays a prevalent role in the trial of Our Lord: "The chief priests and the entire Sanhedrin kept trying to obtain false testimony against Jesus in order to put Him to death" (Mt 26:59). Pilate joins in: "See how many things they accuse you of" (Mk 15:4). When Jesus gives no answer to the gossip, Pilate is "amazed" (Mk 15:5).

Gossip is not found only in Scripture; it is not limited to gardens or Sanhedrins. It is at home in our everyday lives as well — in the grocery store aisle or in the corporate boardroom; on the sidewalk or in the church sacristy: *"Guess what I just heard. You won't believe this ... Do you know how she got to be head of the Home and School Association? She and her husband give a lot of money to the Church, that's how ... at least that's what I heard."* We tend to dismiss gossip as a daily fault that is virtually unavoidable, and generally only a minor bad habit. But it is far more. The devil gets more mileage out of gossip than he does most of the other major sins. Gossip is not merely a minor itch to chatter, or a bad habit. It is a sin, and it opens the door to the devil and his temptations, because gossip imitates the devil in the very first temptation. The little weed of gossip grows quickly into the thorn bush of conspiracy. Gossip comes in many forms: hearsay, rumor, seemingly harmless information-sharing, or even concern for the person we're talking about. But no matter how it attempts to disguise itself, gossip always offends against charity. Gossip speaks about another, whereas charity speaks *with* another.

Gossip does not want to listen. It only wants to hear. It is the chatter that relies on the absence of the one it speaks about. It emerges from rumination and fixation on what we do not have, and cannot get. Gossip cannot survive in the face of truth, so it must go behind the back. Closing the door and whispering juicy tidbits of information about someone behind their back is a grave sin, and when we engage in gossip, we are courting serious spiritual danger.

The danger is that gossip seems to be a sin of weakness. We resolve not to talk about people, then we weaken and "end up" talking about a neighbor, a teacher, or a friend. But gossip is not merely a sin of weakness; it is also a sin of malice. It destroys charity, even as it simply pretends to be a slip. This is why the devil loves gossip, because sins of malice lead us into mortal sin — where the devil's coil tightens to such a degree that life is cut off. From here, he can then lead us further into the coil, so that we are completely cut off from God. As the coils of isolation, the mirror, wondering what others think of us, and gossip tighten around us, they increase their hold. Unaware that we are becoming more and more trapped, we instead believe that we are more powerful, and that we have the right to control things even more. And few things promise the illusion of control as much as dabbling in, or even entering into, the occult.

The Occult: The Devil's Doorway

The more we allow the devil to influence our thoughts using the tactics described above, the more we open ourselves to the serious spiritual danger of the occult. While the occult may seem too obvious a strategy for the devil to use, he knows how to mix evil with entertainment in such doses that our dabbling in it seems innocent — until it damages our life. St. Thomas Aquinas points out that occult practices employ the power of the demons.[13] Whether one engages in occult practices intentionally, naively, or out of ignorance, these practices are a doorway for demons to get a foothold in our life through our free will. Some examples of the occult disguised as entertainment include astrology, New Age, fortune-telling, palm-reading, tarot cards, horoscopes, going to mediums or psychics, black magic or "white" magic, Wicca, witchcraft, crystals,

Ouija boards, pendulums, Rieke, Charlie-Charlie, séances, and ESP. The devil disguises these occult practices as amusement to pull us into evil (see CCC 2116–17).[14] He can even use violent music, violent video games, and violent movies to work his way into our lives.

The Old Testament frequently warns of the connections between the occult, paganism, idolatry, and the demonic. Demons cannot work miracles, but they can do things that exceed human power, knowledge, and experience.[15] God's call is fundamentally a summons away from such things, as we see beginning in the Old Testament. Thus we read in Genesis that Abram was led out of the land of the Chaldeans (see Gn 15:7), a symbol of Abram letting go of belief in astrology and horoscopes.[16] The Book of Deuteronomy cautions against approaching anyone who "practices divination, or is a soothsayer, augur, or sorcerer, or who casts spells, consults ghosts and spirits, or seeks oracles from the dead" (Dt 18:10–11). These practices are often portrayed as a way to know, influence, or control the future through these secret or occult means. When we become obsessed with trying to know the future and use the occult to effect the changes we want, we open the door to demonic influence in our lives.

This is a major reason why these things are so dangerous. Through them, the devil pretends to offer us the tools to do what he tried to do: pridefully control and change the future. But the future is known only to God. Rather than praying to God about the future, those who engage in the occult are seeking to know the future. In doing so, they are committing serious sin by breaking the First Commandment in turning away from God, who holds the future, to another power to "somehow" now know the future and thus get what they want (some form of power, "healing," "answers," or information) as they want it. In this, they also attack the providence of God, refusing to trust that come what may, God will care for His faithful ones. At the same time, they are, perhaps unwittingly, turning to a spirit other than God, and in so doing are worshiping a strange god or idol.

The same is true of those who turn to these methods to "contact" the dead. When we turn away from God, there is only one direction in which we turn. The Book of Deuteronomy continues: "With strange gods they incited him, with abominations provoked him to anger. They sacrificed to demons, to 'no-gods,' to gods they had never known" (Dt 32:17; see Lv 17:7; 2 Chr 11:15). The Book of Leviticus likewise advises: "Do not turn to ghosts or consult spirits, by which you will be defiled. ...Do not recite charms or practice soothsaying" (Lv 19:31, 26). The psalmist says that "For the gods of the nations are idols" (Ps 96:5), but the LXX translation is telling. It reads, "All the gods of the peoples are demons."[17] Even engaging in these occult practices as a prank, for "fun," or out of curiosity is dangerous, because even if we approach them for what we think is entertainment or playful adventure, we are still approaching, if not opening, a very serious door with our free will. Drawing on the theological writer Origen, Daniélou observes grimly: "As long as men worship idols, their devils are all-powerful. Their angels can do nothing ... "[18] Moreover, he reminds us that "St. Augustine follows the general patristic tradition in recognizing a connection between fallen angels and human idolatry."[19]

The prophets, too, are aware of the danger of such practices. Isaiah emphasizes their emptiness: "Secure in your wickedness ... keep on with your spells and your many sorceries, at which you toiled from your youth. Perhaps you can prevail, perhaps you can strike terror! You wore yourself out with so many consultations! Let the astrologers stand forth to save you, The stargazers who forecast at each new moon what would happen to you" (Is 47:10, 12–13; see also 8:19–22 and 2:6). The prophet Zechariah is equally strong: "For the teraphim have spoken nonsense, the diviners have seen false visions; Deceitful dreams they have told, empty comfort they have offered" (Zec 10:2).

The New Testament also presents the evil influence of magic

and the occult. St. Paul affirms this direction and connection: that when we turn to the occult, we are seeking to know things that belong only to God, and offering what is due only to God to the powers that stand behind the occult. St. Paul is emphatic on the connection between idolatry and the evil angels: "I mean that what they sacrifice, [they sacrifice] to demons, not to God, and I do not want you to become participants with demons" (1 Cor 10:20). The drawing of lots was a type of magic.[20] Thus, when the soldiers cast lots for Jesus' clothing at the crucifixion, they are not just gambling; they turn away from the mystery of the cross and abandon themselves to the magical chances of paganism, which is the doorway to further evil. The Acts of the Apostles describes how Simon Magus practiced "magic" and amazed the people of Samaria for a long time (see 8:9–24). St. Justin Martyr tells us very clearly that Simon Magus's magic came through the power of demons.[21] St. Paul was well aware that evil has at its ready disposal "the one whose coming springs from the power of Satan in every mighty deed and in signs and wonders that lie, and in every wicked deceit" (2 Thes 2:9–10; see Col 2:8). He cautions us against being enslaved to the elemental powers of the universe (Gal 4:9). The Book of Revelation decries those who "did not repent of the works of their hands, to give up the worship of demons and idols made from gold, silver, bronze, stone, and wood, which cannot see or hear or walk. Nor did they repent of their murders, their magic potions, their unchastity, or their robberies" (Rv 9:20–21). St. John therefore warns: "Children, be on your guard against idols" (1 Jn 5:21).

One of the false promises of the occult is that it allows us to predict or foretell the future. Even here, the occult is a lie. Angels cannot tell the future. God alone "searches out the abyss and penetrates the heart ... possesses all knowledge, and sees from of old the things that are to come. He makes known the past and the future, and reveals the deepest secrets" (Sir 42:18–19). However, because of their closeness to God and their comprehensive knowledge of the visible world, angels can surmise from cause to effect with stunning immediacy and accuracy. They reflect the wisdom of God, which allows them to "[know] the things of old, and [infer] the things to come" (Wis 8:8). They can grasp a trajectory of likely future events without being able to know the future. The good angels use this ability to teach us about the things of God and to guide us and protect us on our journey. The evil angels, who did not lose this ability in their fall, use it to tempt us. Ultimately, they want us to despair about the future as they have.

Satan hates the future. When he learned that God would become man in the Incarnation, Lucifer was horrified at that future occurrence and did all he could to figure out how to destroy it. His evil actions have all followed from that pride-centered fear. From the moment he learned that, given God's abundant humility and love, God would create man to share His own dignity and would himself become man through the Incarnation, Lucifer did all he could to destroy God's plan.

This is the heart of his rebellion. All sin prior to the Incarnation arose from Lucifer's attempts to avert it. All sin after the Incarnation arises from Lucifer's attempts to destroy its providential and supernatural effects.

Even dabbling in the occult is dangerous. That is why the devil disguises it as entertainment. The occult is the lie that entices us to think we can control the future and other people. A little control is never enough. We want more and more, and so the dabbler quickly becomes a practitioner of the occult. The devil uses the occult as a gateway to gain a deeper foothold and lure us away from God. Yet the "control" we think we gain through the occult is an illusion. The occult is a lie, because in occult practices it is really the devil who takes control, and sooner or later, he will demand his due.

Looking for Guardians

Demons cannot act directly on our intellect or will, so they cannot cause or force us to sin.[22] It is important to always remember that, no matter how cunning he may be, the devil cannot enter the substance of the human soul itself. This area is sacrosanct, and he cannot violate it directly.[23] The devil and his minions ordinarily act on us indirectly by disguising evil as good.

This is why most of the devil's temptations do not invite us to cross a clear line between good and evil. Rather, his temptations are like a coil that catches us, and the more we engage the temptation, the more we get caught in it. When we give in to these subtle temptations, the evil angels can then open up the show rooms of other sins to tempt us further: gluttony, lust, greed, envy, anger, sloth, pride, and vanity. While the angels can act on our external senses, psychology, or passions, they cannot force our will. So instead, they do all they can to persuade us. The more the evil angels can make us grow comfortable with venial sin, harming our relationship with God, the more they receive our permission to continue their work. Cumulative venial sins make it easier for them to tempt us to commit mortal sin, by which we completely break our relationship with God and drive sanctifying grace from our soul. They want us to persist in mortal sin and to die without repenting, so we lose heaven.

This is why discernment is essential. In temptation, we are facing a unique kind of spiritual night. We cannot rely on our efforts alone, or think we can somehow outwit the devil by our own thinking and skill. The only way to outwit him and escape his temptations is to cling to God in Christ Jesus. In His providence, He sends the holy angels to our aid. The good angels are our guardians in the night who guide, teach, and protect us. While the evil angels seek to lure us into sin, the good angels illumine our intellect by presenting us with good choices.[24] As we will explore in the next section, God's assistance for our good acts comes to us through the work of the good angels.[25]

PART III

GUARDIANS IN THE NIGHT:
From the Wilderness to the Resurrection and on to Galilee

Chapter Seven

ALLIES IN THE NIGHT

In the Bible, night, with its threats and dark unpredictability, stands for something more than the chronological time of meteorological darkness between sunset and sunrise. In the Bible, night is a symbol that stands for the chaotic time of spiritual darkness, of sin. The Lord says: "But if one walks at night, he stumbles" (Jn 11:10). St. Matthew tells us that St. Joseph, the guardian of the infant Jesus, protects Him from the darkness of Herod that seeks Jesus' life, and flees with Him to Egypt "by night," when Herod's wrath blazes most intensely (see Mt 2:13–22). Nicodemus comes to Jesus "at night" (Jn 3:2), still caught in the fear of what others would think if they saw him speaking with the Lord. The rich fool in the parable learns that his soul is required of him "this night" (Lk 12:20). Jesus confronts the demons at night in Mark's Gospel: "When it was evening, after sunset, they brought to him all who were ill or possessed by demons" (Mk 1:32). On Holy Thursday evening, the Lord predicts that the disciples will all fall away from him "this night" (Mt 26:31). Holy Thursday night is the precursor to the "hour, the time for the power of darkness" (Lk 22:53). St. Peter betrays the Lord "this very night" (Mk 14:30). When Judas departs the Last Supper on Holy Thursday evening, on his way to betray Jesus, St. John tells us, "And it was night" (Jn 13:30).

After Adam committed the original sin in the garden, we are told: "When they heard the sound of the LORD God walking about in the garden at the breezy time of the day, the man and his wife hid themselves from the LORD God among the trees of the garden" (Gn 3:8). The "the breezy time of the day," or as it is sometimes translated, "the cool of the day," means the evening. Night is falling. On a spiritual level, it means that the darkness has descended now that human beings have sinned. They are then cast out of the garden into the wilderness, and as we shall see, an angel stands guard. This scene repeats itself in our lives, too: The night of sin and temptation leads us to wandering in the wilderness.

Night is the time of peril that can lead to further destruction; the time when the devil makes his move. But heaven is not outdone. The good and holy angels are central to the plan of God to draw us back to himself, which means that night is also the time when the holy angels stand close by. St. Paul urges us on: "But the Lord is faithful; he will strengthen you and guard you from the evil one" (2 Thes 3:3). The Lord himself teaches of the closeness of the angels in the depths of the night in the Garden of Gethsemane: "Do you think that I cannot call upon my Father and he will not provide me at this moment with more than twelve legions of angels?" (Mt 26:53). God sends us the good angels to be our guardians in the night and to assist us, teach us the way of virtue, and protect us in the wilderness and its dark paths.

The good angels know very well what is really going on in the events of our daily life, and how the evil angels seek to throw us off the track and lure us away from God. In the night of this world, we need light, and the holy angels help us to see through the disguise, to discern, and to reject the evil angels. The holy angels are our guardians in the night.

The Cherubim with the Flaming Sword:
The Angel Between the Garden and the Wilderness

After Adam and Eve commit the original sin, God speaks to the angels. And God does not complain or yell or blame human beings. He speaks with care: "Then the LORD God said: See! The man has become like one of us, knowing good and evil! Now, what if he also reaches out his hand to take fruit from the tree of life, and eats of it and lives forever?" (Gn 3:22).[1] The first thing God does after we sin is to speak of His wise and loving plan — a plan that calls on the angels. The angelic mission takes on a particular intensity after Adam and Eve's sin and expulsion from paradise. The first holy angel to appear after the Fall is entrusted with a fearsome task: "He expelled the man, stationing the cherubim and the fiery revolving sword east of the garden of Eden, to guard the way to the tree of life" (Gn 3:24). Just as when the evil angels fell, God separated light from darkness (see Gn 1:4), so too after the fall of original sin, He separated divine light from the darkness of human sin by means of His angel with the flaming sword, who stands between the garden of creation and the wilderness in which human beings find themselves after sin.

God instructs the angel to guard the way to the tree of life, lest fallen human beings reach it and live forever in sin. We human beings do not have an angelic intellect. Our choices are not necessarily permanent until our death. While we live, we can remake our choices. The angel with the flaming sword guards the sanctuary of God and casts light upon the humble, calling them to repent. The flaming sword is not a threat to human beings, but an invitation — a beacon which reflects the glory of God calling out to us. It is only a threat to those who oppose God. The angel with the flaming sword stands for all the good angels who rush to us after sin to protect, heal, and guide us back to the way of light, and help us remain in the life of God's grace.

Light in the Darkness

The light from the angel's flaming sword reappears time and again throughout Scripture, providing comfort to all who seek God. Light becomes the sign of God's presence in the midst of fear: "He spread a cloud out as a cover, and made a fire to light up the night" (Ps 105:39). In the Gospel, light fills the night as the angels of the Nativity likewise reflect the supernatural light. They announce the birth of Jesus to the shepherds keeping watch over the flock near the city of Bethlehem (see Lk 2:13–15). St. Luke tells us: "The angel of the Lord appeared to them and the glory of the Lord shone around them, and they were struck with great fear" (Lk 2:9). Poised to announce the long-treasured mystery of the Incarnation, the angel does not just lift the veil of invisibility and become visible; the angel is illuminated within the overall glory of the Lord. The course of radiant light now brilliantly encircles the shepherds. The angel leads the shepherds, not to contemplate the miracle of the angel's appearance (stunning in itself), but Christ himself. The angels bring the shepherds to keep watch with them in adoration of the very Lamb of God.

Light fills the night again after the resurrection of Jesus, when the angel appears at the empty tomb on Easter: "His appearance was like lightning and his clothing was white as snow" (Mt 28:3). The cherubim's flaming sword has been absorbed by Christ in His passion. Now, at the Resurrection, the dazzling light intensifies as Christ restores the way to the tree of life. The good and holy angels go forth and overcome all that is not of God, even as they overwhelm and transform us to be more configured to Christ.

The power of Christ's light continues after His ascension, as we read in the book of Acts that light flashes around St. Paul in his moment of conversion on the road to Damascus (see 9:1–19). Before he hears the voice of Jesus, "a light from the sky suddenly flashed around him" (9:3). The Greek word for "flashed around" is *periastrapto*, meaning the light of a star (*astra*) streamed close enough to touch him. Elsewhere in Scripture, angels are referred to as "stars" (see Jb 38:7). The unexpected light finally humbles Paul and throws him to the ground, the place from which humanity was originally created (Gn 2:7). Paul later witnesses to the Resurrection and to the existence of angels. He speaks in such a way before the Sanhedrin that the Pharisees wonder, "Suppose a spirit or an angel has spoken to him?" (Acts 23:9).

But for the shepherds, the women at the empty tomb, and St. Paul, the light does not mean their journey is over. In fact, the light leads them deeper into the spiritual wilderness. The flaming sword at the entrance to the Garden of Paradise represents the purgative way of the spiritual life. It is a sign of the abiding protection of God over his people who are journeying in the wilderness. The spiritual heritage of the Church generally recognizes at least three overall stages to the spiritual life. The first is the purgative stage. This is the stage in which God works to purify us from attachments to the world and sin. This stage ordinarily lasts a long time, and is characterized by an ongoing struggle, as we can easily slip back into sin multiple times and reignite our attachments and tendency to sin. After the purgative way, where the angels serve as our guardians, we can more freely continue in the second way, the illuminative way of the spiritual life, where the angels reflect the brilliance of the divine light as God makes known His mysteries in a more intimate way. This paves the way for the third stage of the spiritual life, the unitive stage, in which we are invited very close to God.

Angels in the Wilderness

After they sin, Adam and Eve go from the garden into the wilderness. As their descendants, we are there too, even after baptism, because our nature is wounded by sin. Baptism removes the guilt of sin, but the tendency to sin (its wound) remains in the baptized. As the *Catechism* teaches, "By our first parents' sin, the devil has acquired a certain domination over man, even though man remains free" (407). The wilderness is a place of purification from the tendency to sin, and where we must confront temptation that arises due to this wound left by sin. Yet the angels accompany us as our allies in the wilderness, where our struggle against the devil takes place, where we are "aided by God's grace" (409). The wilderness is not easy. We confront our own frailty and weakness in the wilderness. While we are struggling in the wilderness, it can seem as if we experience one failure after another. The wilderness is a place of loss, regret, and breaking apart. But there is more to the wilderness. The angels assist us there, and they bring a fruitfulness even to the struggle.

Even though it is a place of struggle, the wilderness holds a secret for us. The word for "wilderness" in Hebrew is *midbar*, meaning "the uninhabited place," the place where we are on our own, the place of vulnerability. But there is a deeper root word in Hebrew, *dabar*, which means "to speak a word, converse, promise." There is always something deeper in the wilderness: a promise. The wilderness is therefore a spiritual place, and it is often a lonely place. Angels seek out the lonely — those who wander in the desert wilderness. The Hebrew word for "lonely" is *yakhed*, which can mean "desolate," but more often means "the darling" — the one who is united closely to God. It is precisely in the midst of the turmoil of life — in the wilderness — that God frequently speaks, but He often does so by means of His angelic witnesses so as not to overwhelm us. We tend to want this closeness with God without having to go through the wilderness. And we want the wildernesses of our lives — healing after a betrayal, recovery from addiction, or grieving the emptiness after loss — to be over with the snap of our fingers or the push of a button. But the wilderness experience lasts a long time in the spiritual life, because it is there that the promise is born, where God's word can finally get through.

The wilderness has both a quality of dread about it and a quality of glory; it is the place of the most severe temptations, but also of the highest intimacy with God.[2] It is the place of both the danger of the tempter, and of nearness to God. Hosea says that God speaks to the heart of His beloved in the wilderness (Hos 2:16).

We need angels in the wilderness, in large part because Satan is more disguised there, and he continues to tempt us. He wants to draw us farther from God into sin so that we will make our alienation from God permanent. In the wilderness, we contend with our tendency to sin — what the tradition calls *concupiscence* (see CCC 400, 1707). God can make use of the wilderness to strip other things away, so that we can see the snare of temptation more clearly. In the spiritual wilderness, the angels, our guardians in the night, teach us our responsibility as we face temptation. Often, we think that temptation is somehow our own fault. This is not true; temptation is not our fault. It is, however, our responsibility (Gal 6:4) to learn to be vigilant so that we can confront the near occasions of sin. We also often believe that our response to temptation should be perfect — to make the temptation go away, to conquer it immediately, or to somehow be immune to it in the first place. This is a "secret snare" of the evil one, who tries to convince us that if we can't conquer a temptation immediately, we should simply give in to it. Again, we need the angels to help us navigate and respond to the temptations we face in the wilderness.

Throughout Scripture, God uses His angels to find His chosen ones who are lost in the wilderness. The angels then lead the one they find back to God. The psalmist can therefore say, "He found them in a wilderness, a wasteland of howling desert" (Dt 32:10). Through the work of the angels, God himself becomes our way through the wilderness: "God leads the war in the wilderness for those who belong to him: indeed, he himself is this path."[3] Angels are therefore familiar with the wilderness, and they are ready to meet us and help us there. The angels guide us through the wilderness.

An angel guides and protects the Israelites in the desert wilderness:

> The angel of God, who had been leading Israel's army, now moved and went around behind them. And the column of cloud, moving from in front of them, took up its place behind them, so that it came between the Egyptian army and that of Israel. And when it became dark, the cloud illumined the night; and so the rival camps did not come any closer together all night long. (Exodus 14:19–20)

An angel meets the mother of Samson in the wilderness of her long barrenness and makes a life-giving promise (see Jgs 13:3–22). An angel "[takes] up a position on the road as his adversary" as Balaam seeks to flee the wilderness (Nm 22:22–27). We are told that the angel stood "in a passage so narrow" (Nm 22:26) to confront Balaam on that occasion. The wilderness is full of narrow places — places of challenge. An angel challenges the Israelites in the wilderness of Bokim and makes them face their own infidelity (Jgs 2:1–3). The wilderness can also last a long time: The prophet Zechariah meets the angel among the myrtle trees (Zec 1:8–12) after seventy years of suffering for Jerusalem.

When Hagar flees into the lonely wilderness because of the harsh oppression of Sarah, she meets an angel: "The Lord's angel found her by a spring in the wilderness, the spring on the road to Shur" (Gn 16:7). The guidance of the angel turns the threat of rejection and being forgotten into a promise of new life. The Hebrew word used to describe the encounter between Hagar and the angel means that the angel "discovers" Hagar. Similarly, God's angels often discover us when we are lost in the wilderness with nowhere to turn. Angels also appear to those who do not know which way to turn. Since angels know their way in the wilderness, they can find us when we are lost.

The wilderness is not miles away; we can be in the center of a major city and still stuck in the wilderness. And we do not plan to be in the wilderness. Instead, we usually find ourselves there unexpectedly, as we navigate the difficult paths deep in the inner territory of our heart. The wilderness is a place of temptation where the devil tries to get us to give up on the promises of God, to get out, to escape. He tempts us to go after the quick fix of pleasure to numb the pain we experience — alcohol, shopping, relationships, etc. Or he might tempt us to seek out or cause drama, substituting the real crisis we need to face with a fabricated one that gives us a busy and self-important energy.[4] But pleasure and drama do not heal; they only cover things up and leave us in deeper pain than we were before.

The wilderness is a path: the path of asceticism. We are familiar with ascetical practices such as fasting and almsgiving, but in the wilderness, asceticism is more than a practice; it is a way of life into which we are thrust, the training ground for humility. The asceticism of the wilderness turns our attention back to the mystery of Christ. Just as the evil angels lure us with temptation in the wilderness, the good angels spur us on to discernment, opening up the path of asceticism for us. They are especially adept at this because they know creation through and through, and they know our intellectual nature, but they also know humility.

Just as Jesus was led by the Spirit into the wilderness to confront the lies of the demon, we also go into the wilderness "deliberately to affront [the devil] in order to struggle with him face to face and, according to the word of the Gospel, to dislodge the 'strong man' from his fortress, by the power of the 'stronger man', so as to take away his arms and reduce him to impotence."[5] The solitude of the wilderness is crucial, because there we discover "the obscure powers that are as it were lurking there, whose slaves we inevitably remain so long as we are not aware of them."[6] It is at this point that we must also discover more directly the work and intervention of the good and holy angels. The good angels protect and guide us in our struggle. In the previous chapter, we discussed the five principal coils by which the devil traps us and leads us gradually into sin. In the next chapter, we will explore five distinct paths along which the good angels lead us and introduce us to the humility of Christ.

Chapter Eight

MEETING THE FIVE ANGELS OF HUMILITY IN THE WILDERNESS

The good angels meet us when we are struggling in the wilderness. It is where they teach us the principal act of asceticism: to keep our eyes on Christ. As the psalmist says, "My eyes are ever upon the LORD, who frees my feet from the snare" (Ps 25:15). The holy angels rescue us from the snares of the evil one, teaching us to identify and resist the devil's five coils we discussed in chapter six: isolation, the mirror, concern about others' opinions of us, gossip, and the occult. The good angels untangle the bitterness and lead us by five interconnected paths that form us in the ways of God: humility, affection for the ordinary, accompaniment, silence, and forgiveness.

Elijah in the Wilderness: The Angel of Humility

No less a person than the prophet Elijah found himself in the wilderness. That sounds odd to us, because Elijah was a champion for God. How did he end up in the wilderness? Put simply, he was successful, and his success led him to unimaginable danger. Elijah single-handedly took on 450 prophets of Baal (see 1 Kgs 18:21–46). The odds seemed impossible, but Elijah was confident as he faced the false prophets. In fact, Elijah was so confident that he mocked them. The false prophets called upon their god and received no response. Elijah called upon the true God, and God immediately answered with fire. Then Elijah killed the 450 prophets of Baal.

Immediately after Elijah's victory, "Jezebel then sent a messenger to Elijah and said, 'May the gods do thus to me and more, if by this time tomorrow I have not done with your life what was done to each of them [the false prophets whom Elijah killed].' Elijah was afraid and fled for his life'" (1 Kgs 19:2–3). On the surface, it seems simply that Jezebel threatens Elijah, and he runs away — which is odd, considering that Elijah just single-handedly defeated 450 false prophets. He was so confident as he faced them that he repeatedly and publicly mocked them. So why does Elijah's mood change? Champions do not just run away. There is clearly something within Jezebel's threat that makes Elijah deeply afraid, but what is it?

Recall that Jezebel sends a messenger to Elijah. Judging from Elijah's reaction, the messenger in this instance is no simple courier. Recall that the Hebrew word for messenger is *mal'ak, which* can mean a human messenger, but Elijah's unusual reaction suggests that something more is likely at work. The word *mal'ak* is also often translated as "angel." And since this "angel" carries an evil message in response to the resounding defeat of a pagan god, we can reasonably assume that Jezebel's messenger is an evil angel, a demon.[1]

Elijah had stood his ground against the human false prophets, but one demon is far more frightening than hundreds of false prophets. The threat is "to make Elijah as one of the prophets of Baal," or to kill him. Ironically, the demon is fearful of Elijah. We know this because the devil attacks those whom he fears. But this threat is not only a threat of physical death; there must be something more to make God's warrior suddenly fearful. The threat must be the threat of spiritual death.

Remember the wording of the threat that Elijah received: "do to your life what was done to each of them [the false prophets]." It is more literally stated in Hebrew: that the demon will make Elijah's life as the life of one of the prophets of Baal. At first glance, it seems the demon is simply threatening to kill Elijah, to extinguish his physical life, but the real threat is that Elijah will become like the prophets of Baal, that he will *become in his very spirit a living servant of Baal*. Elijah's fear is not merely a worldly fear of physical death, *but a holy fear of an unholy life*. This can happen only through sin. Even after Elijah's victorious action for God, the devil attacks in the worst way: with pride. More sinister than physical death, the evil angel can generate the temptation to serious sin, and even the bold prophet is not immune to temptation. In fact, the prophet so favored by God is uniquely susceptible to temptation, especially the temptation of pride — and in this case, vanity. This is the constant danger of the life of service in the Church: We begin to think that we deserve the credit for the good that God does through us as his human instruments (see Jgs 7:9; 1 Cor 2:4–5).

Success, especially spiritual "success," is a most dangerous thing. When we are in the wilderness, success is a recurrent temptation. Success tends to isolate us. Remember, isolation is the devil's favorite game. Elijah knows that the evil angel is far more cunning than even 450 false prophets, so he flees to escape the ruses of the evil one. He literally runs for his life, fleeing into the wilderness, deeper into the spiritual battle. Out of holy fear, Elijah searches out God, going "a day's journey into the wilderness" (1 Kgs 19:4). Here, in the providence of God, under the guardianship of the angel in the wilderness, the opposite of the evil prediction unfolds.

Elijah falls asleep beneath a tree. The sleep represents prayer, and the tree foreshadows the cross.[2] This is the place of asceticism. Here, the holy angel appears and nourishes Elijah to go on to meet God. Elijah has to flee to the wilderness and find (or, better yet, be found by) the angel of humility, the guardian in the night of the wilderness, who will help him overcome the evil angel. Only then is he free to go from the wilderness to the mountain, where he will hear, in humility, the tiny whispering sound and experience the presence of the living God (see 1 Kgs 19:10–13). Humility is the refuge the good angels have over the evil angels. Humility is the way out of every trap and coil of the devil, the escape hatch from every temptation. St. Ignatius of Antioch says that by humility, "the prince of this world is overthrown."[3] St. Teresa of Ávila tells us that "the devils have a tremendous fear of that learning which is accompanied by humility and virtue; and they know they will be discovered and go away with a loss."[4] By helping us along the path of asceticism, the good angels train us in humility. They lead us to Christ, who is humility in His very Person.

It is interesting to note that in the midst of all Elijah's bold actions against the 450 false prophets, not one angel is visible. It is only when Elijah is faced with the demon and flees that the angel of humility steps out of the shadows.

Elijah had a lot of results. He conquered 450 false prophets. Focusing on results can be dangerous in the spiritual life. We can look for results and think that experiencing consolations in prayer, always hearing high-power homilies, and feeling like we are really making a difference in a parish ministry are proof of God's presence. While these are good things, results are not a measure of the spiritual life, and can actually isolate us into a pattern of needing more and more "good" results. God doesn't look at results the way we do. God looks for ways to help us find the angel of humility, who guides us away from measurement and the gauging of results so that we are led deeper into the immeasurable mysteries of Christ himself.

Moses and the Burning Bush: Angels in the Ordinary

It may seem that Moses has it all going for him. If you read only the headlines, it appears that Moses manages to be in all the right places at all the right times. The Red Sea parts when he extends his hands over it (see Ex 14:21). He speaks to God "face to face" (Ex 33:11). He receives the Ten Commandments from God (Ex 20:1–17). But if you read the fine print, another story emerges. Moses wanders through his own dense wildernesses, and he suffers far more defeats and dead ends than he enjoys mountaintop experiences with God.

Moses tends to get angry. In fact, his anger gets the best of him one day, and he commits murder and then hides the body (see Ex 2:11–12). When his crime is found out, he runs away, going from the heights of recognition and influence in Egypt to being a wandering outcast overnight. He loses it all and has to go work for his father-in-law in the desert, likely feeling defeated and lonely. It is only then, when Moses is crushed, convinced he is nothing, that he sees the angel: "There the angel of the LORD appeared to him as fire flaming out of a bush" (Ex 3:2). While some Scripture scholars have argued that the mysterious angel of the Lord in the Old Testament is actually God, throughout this book I have adopted the teaching of Pascale Parente and W. G. Heidt, who posit that these appearances are truly of angels, acting on God's behalf.[5] We see this intermediary function of the angel especially played out in Zechariah 1:13, where God speaks to the angel, who then speaks to the prophet. Similarly, the angel appears to Moses in a burning bush in the desert wilderness as he leads his flock of sheep (Ex 3:2–4). But Moses could have easily missed the angel.

Burning bushes are not rare in the desert. The desert wilderness is very warm during the day, but at night it grows very cold. Shepherds and travelers often light fires to stay warm. It was not uncommon for a shepherd to be careless in putting out his fire, and the smoldering embers could be easily stirred up by a wind and carried to a nearby bush. Moses had probably seen dozens of burning bushes in his time. The angel had probably tried dozens of times to get Moses' attention. But this time, Moses looks at the bush. He notices something within the ordinary and expected: "When he looked, although the bush was on fire, it was not being consumed. So Moses decided, 'I must turn aside to look at this remarkable sight. Why does the bush not burn up?'" (Ex 3:2–3).

The good angels know how to use the ordinary things, especially in the wilderness. Moses may have passed by dozens of other burning bushes, but it is only when he takes a second look at the ordinary that he can hear the voice of God. It is only then, when the Lord sees that Moses has turned aside to look, that God calls to him from the bush (see Ex 3:4). It takes patience to see the angel in the ordinary. This patience fortifies us and turns ordinary humility into meekness. Meekness is a rare kind of strength, a gentleness that is purified of anger. Perhaps the angel of patience has been trying to get our attention too. He waits in ordinary things like doing the laundry, waiting in line, and even a small, old, dry bush. Things we pass by every day for years and do not notice make good kindling for angels. They are waiting for us to take a second look so they can lead us beyond the ordinary to meet God.

Gideon and the Mysterious Traveler: The Angel of Accompaniment

Doubt has little to do with reason, but is largely an emotional experience. Most of us experience doubt at some point in our lives. For some people, doubt comes early, especially if they have experienced more than their fair share of the hard knocks, stark realities, and cruel betrayals of life. Even for those who seem to be spared the early traumas of life, the hurts eventually come calling, along with the doubt they can generate.

There is no shortage of things to doubt: our parents, our teachers, the existence of God, or His care for us. If we let it, doubt can help us to mature and hone our gifts. But too often, doubt leads us in one of two directions: Either we rebel against our parents, teachers, and even God, or we fall into a strict and even severe, overly literal adherence to things we were taught by our parents and teachers about our faith. Strict legalism is often doubt's favorite hiding place, because it makes us feel secure and in command. But God does not stop calling us, even in the pain of old wounds and doubt.

This is what happens when God calls Gideon in the Book of Judges. Gideon, a military commander, is very sure of himself. God wants Gideon to lead a battle, but Gideon doubts. He has old wounds, as Israel has experienced many setbacks, and the people are scattered, hiding from the rough oppression of Midian (Jgs 6:2). The people have cried out to the Lord for deliverance (Jgs 6:6), and God responds. He sends an angel who appears to Gideon: "Then the messenger of the LORD came and sat under the terebinth in Ophrah that belonged to Joash the Abiezrite" (Jgs 6:11). The angel, who appears to Gideon to be an ordinary traveler, speaks words of accompaniment to Gideon: "The LORD is with you, you mighty warrior!" (Jgs 6:12). But Gideon doubts and questions:

> "My lord," Gideon said to him, "if the LORD is with us, why has all this happened to us? Where are his wondrous deeds about which our ancestors told us when they said, 'Did not the LORD bring us up from Egypt?' For now the LORD has abandoned us and has delivered us into the power of Midian." (Judges 6:13)

Gideon is resentful and seems to have given up as he argues with the angel. But Gideon is really arguing with himself, throwing a pity-party as he worries about what his own people and the Midianites think of him. The angel does not argue or join in his sulking. Instead, the angel sees something in Gideon that Gideon does not yet see: "The LORD turned to him and said: Go with the strength you have, and save Israel from the power of Midian. Is it not I who send you?" (Jgs 6:14). Even in Gideon's doubt and insecurity, the mysterious traveler sees not just confidence and security, but might. Gideon persists in his grumbling. Each time Gideon restates his doubt, the angel, speaking on behalf of God, speaks words of strength: "Is it not I who send you?" (Jgs 6:14); "I will be with you" (6:16); "You are safe. Do not fear" (6:23).

Gideon doubts, but the mysterious traveler intrigues him. Gideon asks if he can bring the traveler food — meat and unleavened bread or cakes (see Jgs 6:19). What happens next leaves him in no doubt that he has met an angel. The angel leaves a sign. The angel points Gideon to the very center of the angelic world: to Christ (CCC 331). The angel gives a sign of Someone yet to come, a distant echo of the Incarnation, and ultimately of the Eucharist: "The messenger of the LORD stretched out the tip of the staff he held. When he touched the meat and unleavened cakes, a fire came up from the rock and consumed the meat and unleavened cakes. Then the messenger of the LORD disappeared from sight" (Jgs 6:21). The staff is a foreshadowing of the cross, the rock is the altar, and the fire is reminiscent of the cherub with the flaming sword who guards paradise (Gn 3:24). The bread foreshadows the Holy Eucharist.

When the call of God takes form in our life, we often think that all trouble is about to subside. Once we start to pray or join a Bible study group, we think life will finally get easy. The truth is, where the promise of God is, the cross is never far away. Notice that Gideon's mysterious traveler sits under a terebinth tree in his appearance to Gideon. St. Ambrose says that the tree is already a shadow of the cross of Jesus.[6] Angels do not take away crosses, but they accompany us and strengthen us to lift the burden of suffering, even as the angel did for Our Lord in the Garden of Gethsemane (see Lk 22:43). The accompaniment of the angel helps us in the spiritual battle so that we can uncover, even in ordinary circumstances, the humility by which temptation uncoils, by which doubt and fear loosen and unravel. Gideon still has to face many hardships. He will even have to face his tragedies. Gideon has to become, like the angel, a mysterious traveler on his way to Christ.

Zechariah in the Temple: The Angel of Silence

St. Luke tells us that the priest Zechariah is righteous (see Lk 1:5–6), blamelessly keeping all the commandments of God. Zechariah believes all the right things and, moreover, he does all the right things, but there is one thing missing from his life. He had no child, though he repeatedly prays for one.

One day, when Zechariah is fulfilling his duties as priest in the temple, standing "before God" (Lk 1:8) at the hour of incense, an angel appears. Unlike Gideon, Zechariah knows it is an angel right away, and he is troubled by the appearance of the angel. Why would a priest who does all the right things and believes all the right things be troubled by an angel's appearance? The angel even has a reassuring message: He tells Zechariah that his prayer "has been heard" (Lk 1:13), and that his wife will conceive and bear a son.

Yet Zechariah, who does everything right and believes all that he should, who says his prayers devoutly, still wants to be sure. You would think a righteous man, who has believed everything else God has said, would believe now. An angel has appeared to him in the temple! But Zechariah does not believe. Instead, he responds to the angel, "How shall I know this? For I am an old man, and my wife is advanced in years" (Lk 1:18).

As much as he has meditated on God, Zechariah has ruminated even more about what is missing from his life: a child. So now, even when a heavenly being tells him his prayer has been heard, he does not believe. His preoccupation with his own hurt and disappointment blocks out the promise of God. His internal chatter is so loud that while he can hear the angel, he cannot listen to the angel. He is so fixated on his pain that he has given up. While he has done all the right things externally, he has simply been going through the motions.

In response to Zechariah's question, the angel says, "I am Gabriel, who stand before God. I was sent to speak to you and to announce to you this good news" (Lk 1:19). Gabriel speaks of the immediate presence of God. His words are a true and firm testimony that he, Gabriel, gazes into the divine plan, and from that vantage point, Gabriel can help Zechariah drag himself away from doubt. But it will take humility. As God's messenger, the archangel Gabriel conveys a measure of God's light to Zechariah, and this light takes the form of silence: "But now you will be speechless and unable to talk until the day these things take place, because you did not believe my words, which will be fulfilled at their proper time" (Lk 1:20).

Humility turns interior noise into quiet and turns quiet into listening. The help that the angel Gabriel gives Zechariah is the grace of holy silence.

Rather than a long explanation of one proof or argument after another, the angel simply introduces Zechariah to silence. Not the silence of resentment or hostility, not the silence that masks a grudge or that covers the pain of hurt and loss — The angel introduces Zechariah to silence before the mystery of God. Holy silence is a key lesson the angels teach us in the spiritual battle. Such silence disentangles the coils from our heart and releases us to be free for the things of God. Gabriel wants to introduce us, too, to the strength of silence, the healing silence that allows us to truly listen to the messenger of God.

Jacob's Wrestling Match: Angels and Forgiveness

We may think that our families in the twenty-first century are dysfunctional and divided. But we did not invent difficult family life or discover it for the first time, as the Old Testament makes plain. Family life in the Old Testament was no picnic, and, as is often the case now, could be a type of wilderness of hurt and betrayal. When things got bad for a family in the Old Testament, they did not hire lawyers to go after each other in court. Instead, they formed armies to go after each other on the battlefield. Jacob knew well the wilderness of family life. It could be downright deadly. Jacob was chosen by God, but that did not give him a pass in wrestling with the difficulties of family life.

Jacob was no angel. He deceptively stole his brother Esau's birth rite (see Gn 27:1–41), and Esau hates him for it and has even sought to kill him over it. So Jacob flees in exile to Laban (Gn 27:43; 28:5), where he enjoys prosperity for a time. But now Jacob and Laban have had a falling out as well, and Laban pursues Jacob (Gn 31:2–3). This is when Jacob meets the angel — not in church or on his way to Scripture study, but as he is stewing in a big pot of rejection. Rejection is one of our deepest fears and most personal of hurts. Rejection makes bitterness a way of life. Jacob is aching because the bond of affection with his brother has drastically transformed into an ongoing wound of betrayal.

And to top it all off, now God is sending Jacob home to where Esau is — the one whom Jacob betrayed — and Esau is waiting with an army for Jacob's return (see Gn 32:6–7). Jacob knows all about blaming himself, thinking he could control or cure all the mistakes and bad things. Jacob has fought himself so often that he forgets he is fighting himself. It is in the midst of all this turbulence that the angel appears to Jacob — and they get into a wrestling match:

> Jacob was left there alone. Then [an angel] wrestled with him until the break of dawn. When the man saw that he could not prevail over him, he struck Jacob's hip at its socket, so that Jacob's socket was dislocated as he wrestled with him. The man then said, "Let me go, for it is daybreak." But Jacob said, "I will not let you go until you bless me." "What is your name?" the man asked. He answered, "Jacob." Then the man said, "You shall no longer be named Jacob, but Israel, because you have contended with divine and human beings and have prevailed." Jacob then asked him, "Please tell me your name." He answered, "Why do you ask for my name?" With that, he blessed him. Jacob named the place Peniel, "because I have seen God face to face," he said, "yet my life has been spared." At sunrise, as he left Penuel, Jacob limped along because of his hip. (Genesis 32:25–32)

When angels are around, setbacks are never what they seem. And so, the holy angels grapple with brash human beings throughout the dark night. They wound us right in the ego (see Gn 32:25–26; Hos 12:4). Just as the angels assisted God in creating human beings from "the dust of the earth," so they assist God in recreating Jacob in a sense, as the angel wrestles with him on the ground. Jacob is recreated from the ground up. As we saw earlier, the occult, fortune-telling, and astrology seem to offer us the easy way to avoid the pain of the past by being sure about the future. Instead, when we grapple with our own past, like Jacob, we learn forgiveness. The angels teach us to draw upon the grace of forgiveness in the spiritual battle so that we may untwist, by God's grace, the hold that wounds and sin often have upon our heart. St. Paul, a man who spent his fair share of time on the ground, reminds us that forgiveness outwits the devil: "For indeed what I have forgiven, if I have forgiven anything, has been for you in the presence of Christ, so that we might not be taken advantage of by Satan, for we are not unaware of his purposes" (2 Cor 2:10–11).

The angels of the wilderness sit down squarely at our defeats and dead-ends. In fact, the more defeats we have had in life (as the world defines "defeat"), the more numerous the angels who have whisked us along, though we may not realize it. It can take decades for us to discern the presence of the angels who remain near us throughout the disturbances and troubles of life. And it is often only there, when we find ourselves losers, in the last place of all, that they can finally lead us somewhere.

***

The angels of the wilderness, our guardians in the night, teach us the asceticism of humility, of the ordinary, of accompaniment, of silence, and of forgiveness, but not for their own sake. Our guardians in the night lead us so that we will meet *the* Guardian in the Night, Jesus Christ. It is He who confronts the demons in the Gospels. In all of our struggles and spiritual practices, we must always remember that we take refuge in Christ, who is the One who ultimately fights the demons. We turn now to the Gospel account where Christ confronts the demons, so that we may take further refuge in Him.

Chapter Nine

CHRIST CONFRONTS
THE DEMONS

J esus performs many exorcisms in the Gospels, and it is clear
from these accounts that Our Lord's ministry runs far deeper
than physical healing, teaching in parables, or confrontations with
the Pharisees. Daniélou summarizes, "If we look beyond the merely
visible, we see that from the Temptation to the Passion, Christ's life
was a struggle with the Prince of This World and his angels."[1] The
Lord's encounters with the demons convey both the undiluted, direct conflict of the ongoing battle between heaven and hell, and the
resolute depths to which the Lord will go in His relentless determination to heal those afflicted with evil spirits. Jesus "conquers Satan's
territory step by step and pushes his forces back."[2] The *Catechism*
affirms, "The coming of God's kingdom means the defeat of Satan's
... Jesus' exorcisms free some individuals from the domination of
demons. They anticipate Jesus' great victory over the 'ruler of this
world'" (550).

The Demoniac in the Gerasene District
(Mt 8:28–34; Mk 5:1–20; Lk 8:26–39)

The Synoptic Gospels tell us of an encounter between Jesus and the demons, which took place in the territory of the Gerasenes. Geography is important here — in the Bible, geography is never just geography, and here the physical location indicates something deeper. St. Luke explains that Jesus and His disciples had "sailed to the territory of the Gerasenes, which is opposite Galilee" (Lk 8:26). St. Matthew describes it as "the other side" (Mt 8:28) — in Greek *peran*, which comes from the root word to "pierce." Jesus frequently goes forth to this mysterious "other side" in Scripture. It is not some encounter with the paranormal, but Jesus piercing the powers of darkness and sin. In Scripture, the "other side" is the place of scarcity, of confrontation with the powers of darkness and chaos. It is where the disciples forgot to bring bread (see Mt 16:5; Mk 8:14; Jn 6:1, 5); it is the place of "the people who sit in darkness" (Mt 4:15–16); the storm arises as the disciples journey to the "other side" (Mt 8:18, 24; 14:24; Mk 4:35, 37; 6:45, 48; Lk 8:22–23; Jn 6:17–18); it is the place where the Lord meets the Pharisees (Mt 19:1–3; Mk 10:1–2); and, finally, He goes to the other side of the Kidron Valley to the Garden of Gethsemane on Holy Thursday evening (Jn 18:1).

In this encounter, the territory of the Gerasenes is on the other side of the sea. The sea represents primordial chaos; it is the place of the turbulent storm (see Gn 1:2, 6:11—9:29; Jon 1:11—2:10). The Lord, traveling into the midst of the sea, portends a confrontation with the forces of chaos and evil. Notice, as well, that for St. Luke, the Gerasene district is "opposite Galilee" (Lk 8:26). After His resurrection, the Risen Lord will tell the women to instruct His apostles to "go to Galilee" where they will see Him (Mt 28:10; see Mk 16:7). Galilee is the region of the public ministry of Jesus, the place where Jesus proclaims the Good News. The territory of the Gerasenes is the region "opposite" the ministry of Jesus. The layers of meaning are clear: We are about to witness a confrontation with all that is opposed to the Lord.

In St. Matthew's account, we are told that as Jesus and His disciples cross the sea, a violent storm rises up and overtakes them in the boat. The forces of disorder and distress are attempting to force the Lord back as He approaches the region where the demons have taken hold. Yet the signs of His victory begin to mount. As the Lord arrives on shore, He has just "rebuked the winds and the sea" (Mt 8:26). Victorious over the elements, the Lord is also victorious over the fear in the disciples. They now marvel that even the wind and the sea obey Jesus (see 8:27). Further victories await.

As Jesus departs the boat, "a man from the town who was possessed by demons met him" (Lk 8:27). The boat is the symbol of the Church. The Lord steps forth in the Church in her pastoral ministry. According to Luke, the possessed man now lives among the tombs. St. Mark is more direct in his account: He tells us that as Jesus comes out of the boat, the possessed man comes out of the tombs (see Mk 5:2). St. Matthew's version of the story involves two possessed men who are likewise coming forth from the tombs. Matthew's description of the two possessed men emphasizes a certain mockery on the part of evil. One of the earliest times "two" is mentioned in the Old Testament is the saving act of God, in which God commanded Noah to take two of every kind of animal into the ark with him (Gn 7:9). Evil always seeks to insult and mock goodness by cheap parody and imitation.

This confrontation near the tombs is not a coincidence. The Lord tells us that the demons abide in uninhabited places: "When an unclean spirit goes out of a person it roams through arid regions searching for rest but finds none" (Mt 12:43; see Lk 11:24). The Greek word for "water" in this passage is *hydor*, and refers to the rivers, pools, and fountains that abounded when the world was created. Water was the first element that the fallen angels saw God shaping and forming; now the evil angels seek out "arid places." Isaiah is even more graphic, noting that the demons dwell in the wasted ruins of howling emptiness in the desert wilderness (Is 13:20; 34:14; Jer 50:39). St. Peter refers to the "waterless springs … for them the gloom of darkness has been reserved" (2 Pt 2:17). The ecclesial writer Tertullian teaches that the demons seek out the waterless places because they are the enemy of life.[3] They resent water and flee it because they associate it with God. Tertullian maintains that we must therefore permanently abide in the water of life.

Scripture continually upholds the dignity of water. In the creation account, after God separated the waters so that the dry land would appear, water was the first to receive the command to "teem" with life and bring forth creatures (see Gn 1:20).[4] The ancient waters were the seat of the Holy Spirit in the creation of the world. Water is also a sign of life: The Holy Spirit gives shape to the watery chaos (Gn 1:1–2); the stream that wells up in Eden (Gn 2:6) precedes and portends the creation of man from the mud of the earth (Gn 2:7). Human beings are formed, and formed anew, by water. For Tertullian, water is God's chosen vehicle: He transforms water at Cana to inaugurate the proclamation of the Kingdom (Jn 2:1–11); He is baptized by John in the Jordan (Mk 1:9–11; Mt 3:13–17; Lk 3:21–22); He walks on water to show His authority (Mt 14:25); He invites the thirsty (Jn 7:37); He recruits the woman at the well (Jn 4:6–10); He crosses the sea (Mk 4:36); He washes the feet of His apostles (Jn 13:1–12); and water flows from His side on the cross (Jn 19:34).

In this Gospel story, something about Jesus stepping out of the boat, which symbolizes the Church, infuriates and arouses the powers of hell. The Lord is advancing in His mission for victory over sin and death. Even as the Lord comes forth from the boat, from His victory over the elements, the demoniacs come forth from the tombs — from the abode of death. Christ has now stepped from the sea into a place of even deeper chaos. The showdown is about to begin. The demoniac (or demoniacs in Matthew's account) dwell among the tombs, because the devil has fallen in love with death. The Book of Wisdom speaks of the devil as "the wicked" when it says, "It was the wicked who with hands and words invited death, considered it a friend, and pined for it, and made a covenant with it" (Wis 1:16). It is not surprising that those under Satan's power sequester in places fraught with death. The tombs are a menacing place where the threatening decisiveness of death is clear. The demon is therefore drawn to such places where death tears away at life. Bouyer explains, "[The demon] haunts tombs, because there death has definitively, it seems, assured his victory over man."[5]

Matthew explains that the demoniacs are "so savage that no one could travel by that road" (Mt 8:28). The word for "fierce" in Greek is *chalepos*, which comes from the root word meaning "chasm" — it is the bottomless chasm into which Satan and the fallen angels are cast. From this cruel place, the demons brew a fierceness from which they seek to make the way to Christ impassable: "no one could travel by that road." Notice the obstruction: *No one could follow the way that Christ intended to take.* This is what the demons attempt to do to us as well. They seek to throw us off the way of Jesus, even before we take a step onto His path. They want us to take the nearest detour back to sin. And so, Christ himself walks the way … to confront evil and sin.

Luke is careful to point out that though the demoniac haunts the tombs, he is "from the town," or city. The city may turn out, however, to be a far more dangerous place than the tombs. The Greek word that Luke uses is *polis*, which shares the same root as the word *polemos*, meaning "battle" or "war." The power of evil is clear among the tombs, but it is more hidden in the city, and, as a result, can be deadlier. If we dwell in the city of the world long enough, our heart begins to be a place given to rumor rather than truth, to appearance rather than reality, and to noise rather than listening to the humble ways of God. It is interesting to note that when Jesus heals, He will, at times, take the sick person "away from the crowd" as part of the healing (see Mk 7:33). When He teaches the disciples, He does the same (Mk 7:17). In the town, the things of God are easily crowded out and drift away into fantasy, while the edges of the world cut deep. Recall that earlier in Luke's Gospel, the crowded town was too busy to welcome Our Lady and St. Joseph as they prepared for the birth of Jesus (Lk 2:7). Then, as now, the "town" is the place of rumors (Mt 24:6; Mk 13:7; Lk 21:9), the center of frantic and often shady commerce, underhanded accounting, and back-room deals. Grudges multiply in the city, arguments replace conversation, and profits rule the day as people step on one another to get ahead, while less successful people are cast aside in business-as-usual fashion. The man is from the town. It is there that his trouble likely got started.

The demons in this encounter had "taken hold" of the possessed man "many times" (Lk 8:29), such that he was naked and homeless, living at the level of instinct, assaulted by even the natural elements. He had lost the dominion God originally gave to man in Genesis. The man's lack of clothes is significant; it places him in the time immediately after sin, when Adam and Eve were naked and ashamed, prior to God making clothes for them (see Gn 3:21).

Notice that the demons recognize the Lord. Merely seeing Him is enough for them to cry out: "What have you to do with us, Son of God?" (Mt 8:29). The words of St. James ring true: "Even the demons believe that [Jesus is the Son of God] and tremble" (Jas 2:19). The demons recognize the Son of God, whom they contemplated in initial beatitude, and whom they then rejected. This was their original complaint — that the Son of God would take flesh and "bypass" the angelic nature in the Incarnation. Now that they look on the Incarnation himself, the demons raise their hideous complaint again.

The demons know that their fate on earth is to be the same as it was in heaven: The Lord will cast them down again as He did from heaven. So they ask Jesus to cast them into the swine — the source of commerce for the town. The demons are not asking to go somewhere new, but to a place they know well: the way of greed, pride, and envy. The demons came forth from the tombs by their own power, but they depart from the possessed man (or men) not of their own power, but by the Lord's. And He compels them to depart with one word: "Go" (Mt 8:32). The Greek word used here is *hypagō*, the same word by which the Lord drives away the devil in the temptation in the wilderness (see Mt 4:10). The Lord does not engage them in conversation as Eve did in the Garden of Eden. Instead, He speaks one word of command and banishes them. As Balthasar notes, "An absolute authority is needed if the true nature of evil is to be unveiled."[6] The Apostle James reminds us, "Resist the devil, and he will flee from you" (Jas 4:7). The demons go into the swine and then into the sea (Mt 8:32), submerging into the place which the Lord has already brought into obedience (Mt 8:27).

Just as the demons saw Jesus and cried out, so too, the swineherds see the action of the Lord and run away (see Lk 8:34). It is as if the exorcistic action of Jesus has cast the swineherds out too. They go back to the town, the region of worldly affairs, where money talks and shady deals hold sway — the place from which the possessed man originally came — and tell everyone what happened (Lk 8:34). The people from the town now come to see Jesus. The demons saw Jesus and cried out; the swineherds saw the action of Jesus and ran away. Now the town comes out to "see" Jesus, and they also see the man who had been possessed now healed, clothed, and sitting at the feet of Jesus (Lk 8:35).

The possessed man has been restored. He has been clothed, not with garments as Adam and Eve were, but in Christ. But notice the reaction of the townspeople: They are afraid of what they see, just as the demons and the swineherds were before them. They are perhaps more afraid of the possessed man now than they were before, now that they see the man with Jesus (Lk 8:35). The town, the network of the world, is always afraid of healing — and all the more afraid of salvation. The town is a lot like the turbulent sea that the Lord has just crossed over. The sequence before them is now clear: Jesus has cast the demon out of the man and into the swine, which descended into the chaos of the sea and died. Jesus has cast their commerce (that easily ran a cover for greed, envy, and pride) into confusion by calling the man to obedience. He has saved the one corrupted by the shadowy ways of business.

Luke tells us that "the entire population" then "asked Jesus to leave" (Lk 8:37). Notice that two entities plead with Jesus in this Gospel passage: the demons and the townspeople. The demons plead to go into the swine. The people plead with Jesus to leave. They want to cast Jesus out the same way in which He cast out the demon. He goes back to Galilee and sends the once possessed (and now healed) man to the "whole town" to proclaim what God has done for him (see Lk 8:39). The wicked way of the city drove the man to the tombs. Having met Christ, the man is now sent back from the tombs as an evangelist to the city, to carry on the sacred mission of Christ. The exorcism, in a sense, is not finished. It must now extend from the healed man to the entire town.

The Unclean Spirit at Capernaum
(Mk 1:21–28; Lk 4:31–37)
The demons do not only haunt the tombs. The subtlety of the devil is complex and multifaceted, and he can show up in places

we least expect him. This is what happens in the encounter in the synagogue of Capernaum: "Then they came to Capernaum, and on the sabbath he entered the synagogue and taught" (Mk 1:21). At first, holiness seems to abound in the synagogue that day. Jesus and His disciples immediately (*euthys* in Greek — we will see the importance of this in a moment) enter the holy place (the synagogue), in the holy time (the Sabbath), and Jesus, the Holy One, does a holy thing: He teaches. St. Mark points out that "The people were astonished at his teaching, for he taught them as one having authority and not as the scribes" (Mk 1:22; see Lk 4:32).

Yet the Gospel immediately tells us of another presence now in the holy place: "In their synagogue was a man with an unclean spirit" (Mk 1:23; see Lk 4:33). We might think that the unclean spirit cannot step on holy ground, but it is clear from this passage that it can enter and even operate in the holy place. This should come as no surprise, for in the temptation in the desert, the devil himself took Jesus "to the holy city, and made Him stand on the parapet of the temple" (Mt 4:5). Evil always seeks to hang out around holiness and to masquerade as goodness. The devil can recite Scripture better than the wisest Scripture scholar and can rattle off verses from the *Catechism* better than the finest theologian. The good angels are not fooled, however. They recognize evil no matter how clever its disguise. Recall the words of Our Lord as He explained the parable of the weeds in the field to the disciples: "The Son of Man will send his angels, and they will collect out of his kingdom all who cause others to sin and all evildoers. They will throw them into the fiery furnace" (Mt 13:41–42). The enemy treads on holy ground for evil purposes: to sow weeds among the wheat (Mt 13:25, 28). The holy angels are the ones who can identify evildoers who camouflage themselves to blend in and appear holy, and they have the authority to gather the evil forces and expel them from the holy place.

Not all English translations of this passage fully capture the original Greek, which conveys immediacy and sets the pace. The Greek notes that "and immediately [*kai euthys*] there was in the synagogue a man with an unclean spirit" (RSV).[7] Just as quickly (*euthys*) as the Lord went to the synagogue, so too (*euthys*) does evil show up to oppose Him. Here, in the synagogue, the evil spirit now comes on the scene as soon as Jesus begins to teach, so much does the devil fear and want to interrupt the proclamation of the mystery of Christ. It is interesting, and somewhat scary, to note that, as soon as the crowd notices how much Jesus differs from the status quo, how much His teaching differs from that of the scribes, it is just then that the unclean spirit shows up. If the teaching of Jesus were simply the same old teaching as that of the scribes, the demon would most likely have remained quiet. As soon as the crowd sees how much Jesus differs from the scribes, it is then that the demon emerges to disrupt.

The teaching of Jesus is different: It is authentic, as His teaching corresponds to His Person. Authentic teaching meets with resistance. This is important for catechists, parents, and teachers to remember. If the devil was so bold as to interrupt the Lord when He was teaching, how much more will Satan immediately try to derail us when we teach our children, students, and one another. The devil hates the authority and newness of Jesus. True teaching that astonishes the people always threatens the evil one. The Lord frequently criticizes the scribes for their hypocrisy in not practicing the justice and mercy they preach, and for their concentration on appearances rather than on the substance of holiness (see Lk 11:37–54; Mt 23:1–39). His mere presence calls out the scribes and their double lives. In this, the Lord has raised the stakes; holiness always does when it exposes evil.

And not only does the unclean spirit show up, he also cries out (see Mk 1:23–24; Lk 4:33). The unclean spirit immediately interrupts the teaching of Jesus to try to make Jesus stumble.

The very presence of the Lord has caused the evil to be revealed immediately. That Greek word mentioned above, *euthys*, in addition to meaning "immediately," also refers to "straight" or "level." The unclean spirit immediately attempts to deter the Lord from the straight path of which St. John the Baptist spoke (Mt 3:3; Mk 1:3). The devil fears the straight path of the Lord's sound teaching. He fears it not only because of its transformative effect on the people, but also because of its effect on *him, the demon himself.* After he cries out, the demon says, "What have you to do with us, Jesus of Nazareth? Have you come to destroy us? I know who you are — the Holy One of God!" (Mk 1:24; Lk 4:34). And this is why the demon fears the teaching of the Lord: because the teaching of Jesus not only reveals, but also destroys evil.

Notice in this passage, however, that in the face of the authentic teaching of the Lord, the demon tells lies. He loves to make lies blend in with the truth so that they become unrecognizable and lead us astray. The lie is right there in the demon's words, "Have you come to destroy us?" The lie is that the demon phrases it as a *question.* The unclean spirit knows very well that Jesus has come to destroy evil: "Indeed, the Son of God was revealed to *destroy the works of the devil*" (1 Jn 3:8, emphasis added). That which the unclean spirit phrased as a question he should have truthfully proclaimed as a statement of fact.

St. Mark tells us that Jesus responds to the lie of the demon quite clearly: "Jesus rebuked him and said, 'Quiet! Come out of him!' The unclean spirit convulsed him and with a loud cry came out of him" (Mk 1:25–26). The Lord will not allow the lie to stand. He quiets the lie. Notice that the demon attempts to disobey the Lord's command to be quiet, responding instead "with a loud cry." The demon has asserted that Jesus is the Holy One of God, but disobediently resists the command of Jesus. We recall the words of St. John: "Whoever says, 'I know him,' but does not keep his commandments is a liar" (1 Jn 2:4), for, as St.

John writes elsewhere, "there is no truth in him" (Jn 8:44).

The teaching and the command of the Lord has now further revealed the lie and reduced the unclean spirit from lying words to a vicious cry. The unclean spirit has failed to interrupt the teaching of the Lord, for the people regard the events they have seen not only as an exorcism, but as teaching. The account that opened with Jesus teaching in a way that astonished now concludes with the crowd, not simply astonished, but "amazed" at "[a] new teaching with authority" (Mk 1:27). And the result, as is the result with all authentic teaching, is uncontainable and immediate (*euthys*): "And *at once* His fame spread everywhere throughout all the surrounding region of Galilee" (Mk 1:28 [RSV], emphasis added). As we shall see now, the angels at the empty tomb are familiar with what goes on in Galilee.

Chapter Ten

IN THE LIGHT OF THE RESURRECTION

A ngels like gardens. There are three great gardens in the Bible, and angels are very active in each: The angels assist God in the administration of the visible universe, which took the form of a garden (see Gn 2:8ff); an angel strengthens the Son of God in a garden, and legions of angels seek to defend Him in the same garden (Lk 22:43; Mt 26:53); and the crucifixion and Resurrection take place in a garden: "Now in the place where he had been crucified there was a garden, and in the garden a new tomb, in which no one had yet been buried" (Jn 19:41).

The Angels at the Empty Tomb

At the Tomb in the Garden, where Jesus was laid after His cruci-fixion, Satan thought he had finally won — that he had overturned God's plan. Death is the devil's sad solution, and he thought that with the death of the Lord, the Incarnation had been undone. But he wanted to make sure. The officials at the time also wanted to make sure: "So they went and secured the tomb by fixing a seal to the stone and setting the guard" (Mt 27:66). Jesus had been killed and His dead body placed in a tomb. Now they placed 1) a stone, 2) a seal, and 3) a guard over the tomb. Fear is usually redundant. Jesus' tomb was certainly quite secure — and yet, a mere three verses later, we read:

> And behold, there was a great earthquake; for an angel of the Lord descended from heaven, approached, rolled back the stone, and sat upon it. His appearance was like lightning and his clothing was white as snow. The guards were shaken with fear of him and became like dead men. Then the angel said to the women in reply, "Do not be afraid! I know that you are seeking Jesus the crucified. He is not here, for he has been raised just as he said. Come and see the place where he lay. Then go quickly and tell his disciples, 'He has been raised from the dead, and he is going before you to Galilee; there you will see him.' Behold, I have told you." (Mt 28:2–7)

Earthquakes capture our attention. Matthew points out the cause of the earthquake: "For an angel of the Lord had descended from heaven and came and rolled back the stone." The Greek word for "for" here is *gar*, a primary participle in Greek noting not just the fact of the earthquake, but its cause. Henri-Marie Boudon reminds us that angels can cause earthquakes: "They can make the winds blow, the rain fall, the thunder roar; they can raise tempests, cause earthquakes, give abundance and famine, cure and inflict all sorts of maladies, and operate many other things almost in a moment."[1] The earth itself responds to the presence of angels. Now, Christ is risen from the dead. His victory over Satan, sin, and death is definitive. Even as the Lord is risen, the angels descend and begin to undo the trappings of death. At the descent of the angels, the earth itself begins to tremble.

The original Greek conveys a depth to the action: The angel arrives (*erchomai*) and arises — in a sense "follows" Christ's action of rising. That is, the angel has a forward momentum toward (*pros* in Greek) the stone. The earth itself is shattered, as is the seal of the tomb, at the descent of the angel witnessing to the Lord's resurrection. The words of the Psalmist are fulfilled: "He is enthroned on the cherubim; the earth quakes" (Ps 99:1). In one sense, the angel now does to the tomb and to the earth (tears them open, pushes them aside) what Christ has just done to death in the Resurrection; the angel follows upon the action of Christ and does what he sees the Lord doing. And the earth isn't the only "one" that trembles at the presence of the angel.

St. Matthew points out that "The guards were shaken with fear of [the angel] and became *like* dead men." Those who guard the tomb fear angels and become like what they guard: dead. The same Greek root is used for the guards trembling as was used for the earthquake. Worldly guards tremble at heavenly beings. Heavenly guards take over and give new strength to those who seek Jesus: "Do not be afraid [like the guards]!" And the angel then leads the women to a place yet more fearful: "Come and see the place where He lay." The angels have a special affection for the mystery of the suffering, death, and Resurrection of Christ. They even honor the place where the body of Christ had lain, and from which He rose from the dead. The place is holy to them, and they want to illuminate its mystery and draw us into it.

St. Matthew explains that when Mary Magdalene and "the other Mary" go to the tomb of Jesus on Easter morning, the angels at the tomb reveal a further mystery: The angels had clearly been listening to the words of Christ during His public ministry. Notice in Matthew and Mark, the angel recounts for the women the words of Jesus: "He has been raised, *just as He said*" (Mt 28:6; Mk 16:7, emphasis added). St. Luke is most explicit in recounting this mystery. The angels tell the women: "Remember what he said to you while he was still in Galilee, that the Son of Man must be handed over to sinners and be crucified, and rise on the third day" (Lk 24:6–7). The angels had been close by, listening as Jesus taught and explained the Paschal Mystery to the disciples.

The place we perhaps fear the most is the grave. The good angels seek to protect us as we face the pain and fear of death, so that we can truly make the victory of Jesus our own in this life. The angels appear that first Easter to those who are distressed at the death of the Lord, and further perplexed at the apparent loss of His body. St. Luke tells us that the women "found the stone rolled away from the tomb" and "when they entered, they did not find the body of the Lord Jesus." Luke continues, "While they were wondering about this, suddenly two men in clothes that gleamed like lightning stood beside them. In their fright the women bowed down with their faces to the ground" (Lk 24:2–5, NIV). The angels appear just when the distressed women "were wondering about this." The Greek word for "wondering" here is *poreuō* — which means more than just that they were thinking about it or trying to figure it out. This word conveys the deeper sense that this moment was a trial for them in the midst of their journey. In fact, that Greek word "wondering" derives from the word *peran* — to be pierced. The women were pierced with sorrow and distress when they entered the tomb and could not find Jesus. It was only after they were pierced in the trial that they could see angels: "Behold, two men in dazzling garments appeared."

The Resurrection reminds us that Jesus is the center of the angelic world. St. John Chrysostom highlights this beautifully in his reflection on the angels appearing to St. Mary Magdalene at the empty tomb as recounted in the Gospel of St. John:

> But Mary stayed outside the tomb weeping. And as she
> wept, she bent over into the tomb and saw two angels in

white sitting there, one at the head and one at the feet where the body of Jesus had been. And they said to her, "Woman, why are you weeping?" She said to them, "They have taken my Lord, and I don't know where they laid him." When she had said this, she turned around and saw Jesus there. (John 20:11–14)

St. John Chrysostom asks why Mary turns around. She has just asked the angels a question and has not yet heard their response. Why then does she turn around, and why do the angels not respond to her? Chrysostom says, "I think that while she was speaking, Christ suddenly appeared behind her and struck the angels with awe. And when they saw their ruler, they showed immediately by their attitude, their gaze and their movements that they saw the Lord. This is what drew the woman's attention and caused her to turn around."[2] The angels are awed by the avalanche of light in the presence of the Risen Lord. That avalanche of light propels all caught in its radiance to Galilee, to the place of pastoral ministry, to the region of the Incarnation.

"Go to Galilee": Commissioned by Angels

Through baptism, the believer shares in the victory won by Jesus through His cross and Resurrection. Though the devil's power has been broken, he continues to assault us as we seek to abide in Christ. The angels at the empty tomb tell the disciples to "go to Galilee," where they will see Jesus. Galilee stands for the pastoral ministry of the Church. The angels at the empty tomb are giving a commission to the disciples and to us. In "Galilee," we proclaim the Gospel and live the corporal and spiritual works of mercy. How do we take on the task of the angels and walk under their protection, especially when we are confronted by temptation?

St. Augustine tells us that the passion of Our Lord is a "lesson in patience."[3] We endure with Christ, and this endurance with Him allows us to discern with Him. Holy discernment is the opposite of temptation. As we cling to Christ, one of the key aspects of discernment is to learn to recognize the disguises the devil employs. There are four main ways in which we ward off the attacks of the devil and live under the protection of the angels: reverence for the holy names, frequent Confession, attendance at Mass, and prayer.

Reverence for the Holy Names
In temptation, it is essential to prayerfully speak the Holy Name of the Lord Jesus, or the name of the Blessed Virgin Mary, the Queen of the Angels. Prayerfully invoking the name of Jesus is especially powerful: "At the name of Jesus every knee should bend, of those in heaven and on earth and under the earth" (Phil 2:10). The name of Our Lady is also particularly powerful as it is she who, through her Son, cooperates preeminently in the crushing of the serpent's proud head (see Gn 3:15). The invocation of the holy names is an act of reverence for God and His divine plan. The holy angels encourage us in this reverence for God and His designs, because the good angels are themselves always reverent before the mysteries of God, especially those pertaining to the Son of God and His Blessed Mother.[4] The act of faith in invoking the holy names is quite powerful, as the devil cannot bear the humility of the Lord and Our Lady. St. Vincent de Paul said, "The most powerful weapon to conquer the devil is humility. For, as he does not know at all how to employ it, neither does he know how to defend himself from it." Nothing unmasks the devil more quickly than the holy names, and "unmasked, Satan is ruined."[5]

The act of invoking the holy names also stands in contrast to the irreverence often shown to the mysteries of God. Mockery of the beauty of God and His loving plan grieves the holy angels. Our reverence is inspired by them, serves as a form of reparation, and summons a new level of protection from the angels.

Frequent Confession

The good angels seek to motivate us to go to Confession. They want to preserve us from evil and to free us from sin. Lucifer's *non serviam*, his rejection of God, is a kind of anti-confession before God. There are few things the devil hates more than the Sacrament of Penance. The devil knows that in Confession, everything is brought into the brilliant light of God's unending truth. When we avail ourselves of this sacrament, even before it is a confession of our sins, it is a confession of our faith in God to forgive our sins. It is a confession of our faith in the Incarnation and of all the beautiful truths that flow from the Incarnation. This is why the devil never ceases to try to talk people out of going to Confession. And if he sees that he cannot prevent someone from going to Confession, he attempts to get them to approach Confession out of self-love, rather than love of God.[6] Humility horrifies the devil, and the humility necessary to go to Confession absolutely terrifies him.

When he had his choice to make, instead of turning to and confessing the fullness of permanent beatitude, Lucifer chose permanent pride, with all its constant envy and perpetual wrath. And so, when he sees that we are planning on going to Confession, he fears it so much that he will throw whatever he can get his hands on at our good plans and intentions to confess and receive the Lord's mercy. The devil watches. St. Teresa of Ávila remarks that the devil will look "to see who it is to whom His Majesty shows particular love."[7] He takes note when the person who has been away from Confession takes a second look at the confessional. He will remind us of a dozen other busy things we have to do instead: the email we have to answer, the phone call we must return, and everything we need to pick up at the drugstore. He will try to highlight how going to Confession "is annoying to our vanity."[8] He inspires thoughts of worry that the priest will recognize our voice, or raises the question of why we should confess our sins in the first place. One of the devil's greatest pseudo-victories of this age is the sidelining of Confession. Ultimately, he attacks Confession because he wants to attack the Mass.

Even though the evil angels make uproar when we decide to go to Confession, the good angels are at work too. They prompt in us the repeated desire to go to Confession. The good angels help us to avoid worry and concern, and they inspire us to look at the forgiveness we will receive in Confession. The good angels will prompt in our mind the memory of key Scripture passages, or verses from hymns that comfort and rouse us. We should speak to the good angels when we decide to go to Confession, and ask their help and protection. They know how to untangle the devil's disruptions and strengthen our determination and resolve.

Attendance at Mass

The devil's attack against the Incarnation finds its outlet now especially in his attack on the Holy Eucharist and the Mass. "Under the consecrated species of bread and wine Christ himself, living and glorious, is present in a true, real, and substantial manner: his Body and his Blood, with his soul and his divinity" (CCC 1413). St. Athanasius says that it is the precious Blood of Jesus that allows us to escape the destroyer.[9] The Eucharist is the nourishment we receive to witness Jesus, and it is also protection from the devil. This does not mean that if we are faithful to Mass, then nothing bad will ever happen to us. But it does mean, in the words of the anonymous author of the *Cloud of Unknowing*:

> Trust God's faithfulness. When you truly turn your back
> on the world to serve him, he will never disappoint you,
> whoever you are. God always provides one of two things
> (without your help): either an abundance of what you

need or the physical stamina and spiritual patience to endure its absence. What does it matter what we have?[10]

He gives us this through the Eucharist.

The devil fears the Mass, especially when we attend daily Mass. At Mass, we adore the Lord and participate in His saving redemption. The *Catechism* reminds us that "Victory over the 'prince of this world' was won once for all at the Hour when Jesus freely gave Himself up to death to give us his life" (2853). The Mass is our sharing in Christ's victory. During Mass, we also join with the angels in giving praise to God (see CCC 335, 1352), and they protect us. At Mass and in Eucharistic Adoration, we remain with Christ in His passion. At Mass, we also pray together with the whole Church for deliverance from evil when we pray the Our Father together (2850).

The holy angels remind us frequently of the obligation and even the desire to go to Mass. The good angels summon from our memory the simple faith of being close to God. They use the examples from the lives of the saints, and even the good example of people we know who go to Mass, to prompt us to step closer to the mystery of Jesus and the Sacrifice of Calvary to which we are made present when we go to Mass. There is an angel set over every church building and every altar to protect it as a heavenly guardian for the community and to offer fitting worship.[11] As we enter the church building, we should greet the angel of that sanctuary and invite their intercession.

Prayer

St. Teresa warns that the devil wants us to abandon prayer.[12] Devotion to the angels is often the missing link in our spiritual lives. The good angels carry our prayers to God (see Rv 8:3–4). The holy angels prompt us to pray grace before meals, to pray before going to sleep, and to pray to seek God's grace before a test. They inspire us to pray for the sick, to offer a prayer when we hear a siren from an emergency vehicle nearby, and to simply pray to be with God out of love. Their reminders help us to form the good habit of prayer.

Of particular help in forming the practice of prayer in our life is prayer to the angels themselves. Prayer to our guardian angel and to the archangels is especially important. Adrienne von Speyr assures us that "[A] Christian is never alone in temptations. Angels are always present to help him, whether he sees them or not. They can take on various, sometimes tangible forms, such as good thoughts or the strength to resist; they can prompt our will not to give in to temptation."[13] The angels are close by — like coaches in prayer who comfort and strengthen us in our prayer life.

Making the Sign of the Cross is a simple yet powerful prayer, which dates to the earliest days of Christianity and explicitly exorcises and casts away the devil.[14] Prayer and devotion to our patron saints is another key recourse for protection from evil. St. Thomas even points out that by special dispensation, it is at times granted to the saints to coerce the demons.[15] St. Joseph is a particularly powerful patron in our struggle against evil. One of his titles is "terror of demons." Praying with Scripture is also a strong protection against the repeated attacks of the devil. The psalms, especially in the Liturgy of the Hours, "are recited in order to confound the demons and neutralize their effects in the soul, as well as to encourage repentance."[16] We find verses in Scripture that we can use to remind us of the victory of Christ and to drive away the assault of the devil. For example: "The foe is destroyed, eternally ruined" (Ps 9:7, Revised Grail Psalms); "Depart from me, you wicked, that I may keep the commandments of my God" (Ps 119:115).

One of the devil's tricks is to make time compete with prayer. He does this especially with the Rosary, because he fears it so much. Pope St. John Paul II said that the accuser never stops in his attempts to devalue the Rosary.[17] Sacramentals such as blessing with holy water and the use of sacred objects such as the crucifix and holy images are also fundamental in our battle against the evil one.

As we draw close to the angelic witnesses at the empty tomb and labor in the field of pastoral ministry in the Church, we are most likely going to experience even further persecution. We now turn to an example from the Acts of the Apostles on how the angels comfort us in times of persecution, knowing that "The angel of the LORD encamps around those who fear him, and he saves them" (Ps 34:8).

In Times of Persecution:
The Angel in Peter's Prison Cell

King Herod was a violent man. He was especially violent toward Christians, even after the Resurrection of Jesus, so much so that he "laid hands" (Acts 12:1) upon the members of the Church. In the Acts of the Apostles, Herod stands for Satan. The devil hates the Church. After the Ascension of Our Lord, when he can no longer attack Christ directly, Satan turns his violent attack against the Church, an attack which can come from forces external to the Church or from forces within.[18] Daniélou reminds us that "The powers of evil which were destroyed by the cross of Christ retain the appearance of effective hostility until the Second Coming."[19] St. Ambrose makes an important distinction in noting that Christians have visible enemies, but that the more serious assaults come from invisible enemies:

> The persecutors who are visible are not the only ones. There are also invisible persecutors, much greater in number. This is more serious. Like a king bent on persecution, sending orders to persecute to his many agents, and es-

tablishing different persecutors in each city or province, the devil directs his many servants in their work of persecution.[20]

At this point, the devil's rage comes from his inwardly knowing he is beaten, but being driven by his insatiable pride to destroy all he can. Pride always thinks that somehow it can undo its own defeat.[21]

Herod, goaded by Satan, attacks the Church to embitter her members. Recall that bitterness is one of the devil's major tools. He uses bitterness and hostility to wreak division. Bitterness stands in the way of forgiveness and is always part of the devil's plan, so much so that St. Benedict reminds us in his Rule that the devil is a bitter spirit: "Just as there exists an evil fervor, a bitter spirit, which divides us from God and leads us to hell, so there is a good fervor which sets us apart from evil inclinations and leads us toward God and eternal life."[22] In his drive to embitter the Church, Herod kills the apostle James (see Acts 12:2). By encouraging Herod to wield the chaos of death, Satan seeks to cause bitterness, division, and estrangement in the Church.

Then Herod turns his hideous wrath toward Peter. Herod takes no chances even with a fisherman-turned-preacher, and has Peter thrown in jail (see 12:3). He sets four squads of soldiers to guard him and has him bound, not with one set of chains, but with two (12:4, 6). Herod's tactics come in layers. Manipulation and fear always do. Herod wants the Church to have nowhere to turn, to be in chaos, turned inside-out and upside-down in anguish. Then, on the night before Herod plans to judge Peter, when things seem at their worst, an angel appears to Peter: "Suddenly the angel of the Lord stood by him and a light shone in the cell. He tapped Peter on the side and awakened him, saying, 'Get up quickly.' The chains fell from his wrists" (12:7). Notice that three things take place as the angel appears in that cell.

First, Scripture tells us that the angel suddenly and instantly appeared in Peter's prison cell: "Suddenly the angel of the Lord appeared." The sense of the Greek word for "appeared" indicates no fleeting presence, but a firm presence. The sense of the Greek is that the angel is at hand, ready and now established in that cell — made manifest. In other words, *it seems the angel was there all along.* The angel was there when Peter was arrested, when the prison cell clicked behind him, when the four squads of guards took their places, and when the double chains were secured. The holy angel by Peter's side has seen all the suffering and been with Peter in that suffering. In the cell, the angel simply becomes visible to Peter. The bars, the locks, the four squads of soldiers, the weapons, and the double chains are no match for the angel sent by God. The angel stands near Peter when no one else could.

Second, "a light shone in the cell." The first words of Genesis resound: "Let there be light" (Gn 1:3). Again, the Greek reveals a deeper reality at work: The brilliance of purity stands forth and is manifest in the rays of light in the cell. Something is brought forth and declared by the resplendent light that can reach the depths of the mind, even through iron bars. The angel is teaching Peter (and us) by this light.

Third, the angel "tapped Peter on the side and awakened him." The angel reaches out from the center of the heavenly light and strikes Peter's side. The Greek word used here can mean a gentle tap, but it can also mean to strike down. It is as if the angel strikes Peter's side in the way in which Our Lord's side was struck on the cross (see Jn 19:34). The tap on Peter's side is a piercing, an incorporation into Christ. With this strike on the side, the angel is continuing Peter's mystical configuration to Christ. Peter's old self is dying, and his new self is rising. It is only after the appearance, the light, and the striking of his side by the angel that the chains fall away. Herod meant those chains to contain the threat of Christianity, and the good angel simply makes those chains fall away. In the presence of the angel, they are now powerless and ineffective.

Fittingly, Peter hears the voice of the angel telling him to get up quickly. Peter must now stand forth as the angel has done by appearing. Configured now more fully to Christ, Peter must become even more visible. The angel's command is the same Greek word used in the command given by the Lord in the Garden of Gethsemane on Holy Thursday evening: "Get up and pray" (Lk 22:46). The angel only reiterates the command of Christ. Notice also that the angel is confident. He does not fearfully rush Peter from the cell in a suspenseful panic: "The angel said to him, 'Put on your belt and your sandals.' He did so. Then he said to him, 'Put on your cloak and follow me'" (Acts 12:8). The angel boldly takes his time and allows Peter to dress himself. But these are not mere details; on the contrary, there is a priestly echo to this action. The angel recognizes Peter's priesthood, conferred on him by the Lord at the Last Supper. In the Old Testament, after their priestly anointing, the priests girded themselves (see Ex 29:9). And so, the angel guides Peter in the routine of his priesthood, even here, even in prison. Peter's ordination is at the Last Supper, but his anointing is one of endurance and of suffering for the Lord. The angel supports Peter in this call to enduring perseverance in imitation of Christ. Peter girds himself for the priestly journey. Likewise, the angel is assisting Peter in fulfilling the prophecy of the Lord: As Christ said, Peter now girds himself (Jn 21:18), but one day will suffer more and be led by another. Through even these seemingly incidental gestures, the angel is revealing the mysteries.

Peter believes at first that he is seeing a vision, but he quickly realizes that the angel he sees is not merely a vision or a hallucination. It is real — in Greek *alēthēs,* "the truth" (see Acts 12:9, 11).

The angel is truly present and visible. And what the angel is doing is true; the angel speaks the truth, that Christ conquers even the vicious chains and prisons of this world. The angel walks Peter, as if in procession, past the first and the second guards (Acts 12:10). The iron gate leading to the city then "opened for them by itself" (Acts 12:10). As with the chains, the iron bars release. Even an inanimate object is moved by the power and intervention of the angel. It is only then that the angel becomes invisible again.

Peter then says, "Now I know for certain that [the] Lord sent his angel and rescued me from the hand of Herod" (Acts 12:11). Peter reiterates the truth (*alēthēa*) that the Lord had sent His angel to rescue him, but in the Greek, the word for rescue here is complex. The Greek is *exaireō*, which has a much deeper meaning than simply setting free from confinement or getting someone out of a difficult or dangerous situation. *Exaireō* means to draw one out, to elevate, to lift or raise up, and to take to oneself, to prefer and choose a person. God is always reaching out to rescue us through His holy angels. Angels rescue us not in the sense that they make everything turn out OK or prevent bad things from happening. So often, we want the angels to intervene on our terms, to fix things, to take us back to the way things were before our trouble and sorrow. Because we so narrowly define rescue, we miss the angels because we are looking for a different outcome. To be rescued does not mean bad things do not happen. If this were true, then Peter would never have been crucified later. To be rescued means that when bad things do happen, we can rest assured that God has not abandoned us, but is with us and has sent us His angels to bear us up and take us to himself.

MISTAKEN FOR ANGELS

A fter the angel freed him from prison, Peter went to "the house of Mary, the mother of John" (Acts 12:12). He knocked, and when they heard his voice at the door, those inside the house said, "It is his angel" (Acts 12:15). Peter had been configured to Christ, and even those closest to him now mistook him for an angel.

Earlier in the Acts of the Apostles, when the crowd attacked St. Stephen as he preached about Christ, the leaders stirred up the people to tell lies about Stephen and accuse him falsely. In the midst of that persecution, something happened: "All those who sat in the Sanhedrin looked intently at him and saw that his face was like the face of an angel" (Acts 6:15).

At the very beginning of Jesus' earthly life, the shepherds of the Nativity went to Bethlehem at the word of the angel and found the Holy Family. Immediately after they encountered the infant Jesus, "The shepherds returned, glorifying and praising God for all they had heard and seen, just as it had been told to them" (Lk 2:20). The shepherds take on the task of the holy angels: They praise God for all that had been told them.

Remember that the members of the Sanhedrin, as they were

persecuting St. Stephen, saw that his face resembled that of an angel (see Acts 6:15). Likewise, St. Peter knocking at the door was thought to be an angel (Acts 12:15). The shepherds of the Nativity take on the task of the angels and proclaim the newborn Christ (Lk 2:17). Their mission is so bound up with the angels' message and the presence of the angels that they are almost indistinguishable from angels. We might never end up behind bars for Christ, though some may tell lies about us because of our faithfulness to Jesus. We might not be asked to shed our blood, but we will likely be persecuted in some way for being a Christian. When that happens, it is important to remember that the angels are closer to us than our persecutors are.

The angels give a commission to all who have met Jesus in His cross and Resurrection through the sacraments. They tell us to do what they do: to plunge back into the wilderness and make the mystery known to others, to proclaim what the angels have themselves made known: the mysteries of the Incarnation and of the suffering, death, and resurrection of Jesus.

What light is to the eye, the good angels are to the soul. We have traveled together through these pages from the garden to the wilderness, from the wilderness to the empty tomb, from the empty tomb to Galilee. Even as we close this book, the good angels gather close and continue to be our faithful guardians in the night as we make known all we have heard and seen.

ACKNOWLEDGMENTS

My gratitude goes first to Most Reverend Nelson Perez, Archbishop of Philadelphia, who kindly assigned me to a sabbatical from November 2020 to March 2021, which allowed time for the completion of this book. The sabbatical took place at Curley Hall on the campus of The Catholic University of America. I am most thankful to Reverend Raymond Studzinski, OSB, director of Curley Hall, and to the priest community there, including my good friend Rev. Msgr. Ronny Jenkins, Dean of the School of Canon Law, for their gracious welcome and kind hospitality during those months. The reflective quiet, prayerful atmosphere, and rejuvenating fellowship at Curley Hall provided the optimum setting for the completion of this manuscript.

These pages were accepted for publication during my time in ministry at Mother of Divine Providence Parish in King of Prussia, Pennsylvania. I am deeply grateful to Reverend Martin Cioppi, Pastor, and for the dedicated staff and parishioners who welcomed me so warmly.

I am especially indebted to Msgr. Thomas Flanigan and the excellent parish team and parishioners at St. Joseph Parish, Aston, Pennsylvania, where I am privileged to serve as Pastor, for their prayers, support, and encouragement.

The invaluable expertise of the team at OSV was a great inspiration to me. I am especially appreciative of my editor, Mary Beth Giltner, and all of her colleagues at OSV who helped bring this book to its publication.

Finally, I am grateful to my sisters, brother, and all the friends who encourage me on the journey and who provide constant support, not only for my efforts at writing, but more importantly for my ministry as a priest.

NOTES

Introduction

1. St. Augustine, *Enarrationes in Psalmos*, 95, 7.

2. H. M. Boudon, "An Exhortation to the Love and Honour of the Holy Angels," in *The Glories of the Holy Angels.*

3. Jean Daniélou, *Origen* (New York: Sheed and Ward, 1951), 239–240.

4. This book deals with the devil's attacks via the means of temptation and sin. The current work does not purport to address the Rite of Exorcism, demonic possession, obsession, vexation, infestation, or infiltration (see CCC 1673 and Ronny Jenkins, "History, Discipline, and Ritual with Regard to Major Exorcisms in the Western Church," *The Jurist* 2001: 1–2, 90–133).

5. Jean Daniélou, *The Angels and their Mission* (Texas: The Newman Press, 1957), viii.

6. St. Gregory the Great, *Forty Gospel Homilies* 34.7 (285).

7. Clement I to the Corinthians, Cap. 30, 3–4:34, 2–35, 5: Funk 1, 99, 103–105.

Chapter One

1. St. Hilary, *Lib.* 2, 1, 33, 35: PL 10, 50–51, 73–75.

2. Daniélou, *The Angels and their Mission,* vii.

3. See Martin Schleske, *The Sound of Life's Unspeakable Beauty* (Grand Rapids, MI: Eerdmans, 2020), 108.

4. Thomas Aquinas, *Summa Theologiae*, I, q.64, a.4.

5. See his *Homilies on Job*, 2.1.6; *Patrolia Orientalis* (Turnhout, Belgium: Brepols, 1903); 42.1:84; see Psalm 82:1: "God takes a stand in the divine council" and Psalm 89:7: "Who in the skies ranks with the Lord? Who is like the Lord among the sons of the gods?"

6. St. Gregory the Great, *Morals on the Book of Job* (Lectionary

Central edition), Vol. 1, Bk. 2, section 3; see also Pascal Parente, *The Angels: Catholic Teaching and Tradition* (Charlotte, NC: TAN, 2013), 3.

7. St. Gregory the Great, *Morals on the Book of Job*, Vol. 1, Bk. 2, section 4.

8. Bonino, *Angels and Demons*, 209, n. 57; Aquinas, *ST*, I, q.63, a.8.

9. Heinrich Schlier, *Principalities and Powers in the New Testament* (Edinburgh: Nelson, 1961), 33.

10. Hans Urs von Balthasar, *Theo-Drama: Theological Dramatic Theory IV: The Action* (San Francisco: Ignatius Press, 1994), 145.

11. St. Gregory the Great, *Morals on the Book of Job*, Vol. 1, Bk. 2, section 6.

12. Ibid., sections 65–66.

13. Charles Moeller, Introduction to Bernard Leeming, SJ, and Walter Farrell, OP, *The Devil* (New York: Sheed and Ward, 1957), 7.

14. St. Gregory the Great, *Morals on the Book of Job*, 2.65.66.

15. See St. John Chrysostom, *Commentary on Job, Patristische Texte und Studien* (New York: de Gruyter, 1964), 35:19; 1.10.

16. Parente, *The Angels: In Catholic Teaching and Tradition, 139.*

17. Aquinas, *ST*, I, q.113, a.2, sed contra; see a.4 sed contra, and I, q.57, a.2, sed contra.

18. Hans Urs von Balthasar, *Theodrama Theological Dramatic Theory II: Dramatis Personae: Man in God* (San Francisco: Ignatius Press), 60–61.

19. Jean Daniélou, *The Lord of History* (New York: Meridian Books, 1968), 31.

20. St. Clement of Alexandria, *Strom.*, 5, 11.

21. See St. Bonaventure, *Commentary on the Gospel of Luke*, Chapters 9–16. Ed. Robert J. Karris, OFM, Volume VIII, Part 2 (New York: Franciscan Institute Publications, 2003), 902.

Chapter Two

1. H. M. Boudon, "The Angels Help Us in Temporal Things," in *Devotion to the Holy Angels*. The Swiss mystic Adrienne von Speyr

curiously notes, "There will in fact always be some people who see angels with their eyes" as in her *Water and Spirit: Meditation on Saint John's Gospel 1:19–5:47* (San Francisco: Ignatius Press, 2019), 39.

2. Aquinas, *ST*, I, q.50, a.1, sed contra. Clement of Rome, Jacob of Sarug, and John of Damascus translate this verse in similar fashion (I Clement, 36, in H. W. Holmes, ed. *The Apostolic Fathers* 2nd ed, trans. J. B. Lightfoot and J. R. Harmer [Michigan: Baker, 1989]; Jacob of Sarug, *On the Establishment of Creation Message of the Fathers of the Church*, ed. Thomas Halton [Minnesota: The Liturgical Press, 1983], 9:194; John of Damascus, *Orthodox Faith, Fathers of the Church: A New Translation* [Washington, D.C.: Catholic University of America Press, 1947], 23).

3. St. John Cassian, *The Conferences* VII, XIII.2, Ramsey edition, 256; see Bonino, *Angels and Demons*, 114 and Parente, *The Angels in Catholic Teaching and Tradition*, 17, 23.

4. St. John Cassian, *The Conferences* VII, XIII.2, Ramsey edition, 256.

5. Henri-Marie Boudon, *Devotion to the Holy Angels*, First part. "The Admirable Perfections of These Blessed Spirits," 3

6. Stanzione, *Essential Guide to Angels*, 39.

7. *The Letters of J. R. R. Tolkien, Selected and Edited by Humphrey Carpenter* (Boston: Houghton Mifflin Company, 1981), 66.

8. Aquinas, *ST*, I, q.113, a.6, r.3.

9. Ibid., I, q.51, a.2, r.1. See Pope St. John Paul II, August 6, 1986.

10. Parente, *The Angels: In Catholic Teaching and Tradition*, 41.

11. Aquinas, *ST*, 1, q.113, a.1, r.3.

12. Ibid., I, q.51, a.2.

13. Origen, *Homily on Luke*, 12.

14. Jean Daniélou, SJ, *The Angels and Their Mission: According to the Fathers of the Church* (Texas: Christian Classics, 1957), 3.

Chapter Three

1. St. Augustine, *City of God, Book XI, Chapter IX* (FOTC 14:201); *Literal Meaning of Genesis IV*, 21:38; I, 9:17 (ACW 41:129);

S.T. Bonino, *Angels and Demons,* 53.

2. St. Basil the Great, *Hexaemeron I.5, Fathers of the Church: A New Translation* (Washington, D.C.: The Catholic University of America Press, 1947), 46:8–9. See also G. Pelland, "Genesis," in *Encyclopedia of Ancient Christianity,* Vol. II (Illinois: IVP Academic, 2014), 109.

3. As in Stanzione, *Essential Guide to Angels,* 40; John Scotus Eriugena, the ninth-century Irish theologian, teaches that the angels are light in the sense that they are a perceptible presence that draws human beings to God, as in *Angelic Spirituality: Medieval Perspectives on the Ways of Angels, Classics of Western Spirituality* (New Jersey: Paulist Press, 2002), 17, 35, and 89.

4. Louis Bouyer, *The Meaning of the Monastic Life* (New York: P. J. Kenedy & Sons, 1950), 28; Cassian agrees; see *The Conferences VIII, VII.1;* Ramsey edition, 295; see Bonino, *Angels and Demons,* 172; Parente, *The Angels: In Catholic Teaching and Tradition,* 5; Pope St. John Paul II, Wednesday Catechesis, July 9, 1986.

5. Aquinas, *ST,* I, q.57, a.1

6. Pope St. John Paul II, Wednesday Catechesis, July 9, 1986.

7. See Parente, *The Angels: In Catholic Teaching and Tradition,* 8.

8. Marcello Stanzione, *Essential Guide to Angels* (Roma: Libreria Editrice Vaticana, 2012), 38–39.

9. See Hans Urs von Balthasar, *The Glory of the Lord: A Theological Aesthetics VII: Theology — The New Covenant,* 355.

10. Eriugena, *Angelic Spirituality,* 17, 35 and 89.

11. St. Dionysius, *Celestial Hierarchies,* xiv.

12. Aquinas, *ST,* I, q.50, a.3.

13. Thomas Gallus, *Extract on the Celestial Hierarchy, Chapter 14,* as in *Angelic Spirituality: Medieval Perspectives on the Ways of Angels in The Classics of Western Spirituality* (New Jersey: Paulist Press, 2002), 234.

14. H. M. Boudon, *Devotion to the Holy Angels,* Third Part. "All the Angels are Employed in the Service of Man," 1.

15. Aquinas, *ST*, II q.1, a.1, see *Bonino, Angels and Demons*, 266.

16. *The Letters of J.R.R. Tolkien, Selected and Edited by Humphrey Carpenter* (Boston: Houghton Mifflin Company, 1981), 99.

17. St. Albert the Great, *Super Dionysii Mysticam Theologiam*, Chapter I, pp. 462.5–11.

18. St. Augustine, *The City of God,* 10.15; 10.17.

19. Alan of Lille, *Treatise on the Angelic Hierarchy* in *Angelic Spirituality*, 207.

20. See the "General Introduction" in Ibid., 31.

21. See St. Bernard of Clairvaux, *Sermones super Cantica*, 31.5 and 1:222.

22. St. Dionysius, *Celestial Hierarchies, IV;* Aquinas, *ST*, I, q.111, a.1, sed contra.

23. Origen, *Homily on Joshua*, 23.

24. St. Basil, *Hom. In Ps.* 33:6.

25. St. Justin, *Second Apology 5.2* (ANF 1:190a).

26. See Bonino, *Angels and Demons*, 84.

27. St. Irenaeus refers to God as like an architect in *Against Heresies Lib.* 4, 14, 2–3; 15, 1:SC 100, 542–548.

28. See Bonino, *Angels and Demons*, 54–55.

29. Bouyer, *The Meaning of the Monastic Life,* 28. See also Balthasar, *Theodrama Theological Dramatic Theory II: Dramatis Personae: Man in God*, 182.

30. John Cassian, *Conferences VIII,* Chapter VII.

31. Origen, *Homily on Jeremiah* 10, 6 as in *Jean Daniélou, Origen* (New York: Sheed and Ward, 1955), 224.

32. St. Augustine, *Eighty-Three Disputed Questions*, Q. 79; St. Augustine, *De Trinitate,* III, 4, 5; see Aquinas, *ST*, I, q.110, a.1.

33. Origen, *Josue,* Hom. 23.

34. St. Gregory the Great, *Dialogue IV, 6.* see Aquinas, *ST*, I, q.110, a.4.

35. Aquinas, *ST*, I q.110 a.1, ad.3.

36. Jean Daniélou, *God and the Ways of Knowing* (San Francisco: Ignatius Press, 2003), 35.

37. Pope St. John Paul II, Wednesday Catechesis, July 30, 1986; see also Parente, *The Angels: In Catholic Teaching and Tradition*, 6, *130–131*.

38. St. Umiltà of Faenza, Sermon Four On the Holy Angels as in *Angelic Spirituality*, 151.

39. As in Parente, *The Angels in Catholic Teaching and Tradition*, 26.

40. Stanzione, *Essential Guide to Angels*, 35–36.

41. Walter Farrell, OP, *The Devil*, 32.

42. Daniélou, *Angels and their Mission*, 3.

Chapter Four

1. Aquinas, *ST*, I, q.62, a.1.

2. Ibid., a.5; See Bonino, *Angels and Demons*, 231–232; Parente, *The Angels: In Catholic Teaching and Tradition*, 43–44; Walter Farrell, OP, *The Devil*, 18–19, 23–24.

3. See Parente, *The Angels: In Catholic Teaching and Tradition*, 44.

4. St. Augustine, *The Confessions,* Book XIII: "On Finding the Church in Genesis I," trans. Henry Chadwick (Oxford, UK: Oxford University Press, 2009).

5. Boudon, *Devotion to the Holy Angels*. First Part. "The Admirable Perfections of these Blessed Spirits," 2; see also Parente, *The Angels: In Catholic Teaching and Tradition*, 26–28.

6. St. Faustina, *Diary Divine Mercy in My Soul* (Notebook V), 1332.

7. See Pope St. John Paul II, Wednesday Catechesis, July 23, 1986.

8. See Aquinas, *ST*, I, q.62, a.5, r.1.

9. Matthias Scheeben, *The Mysteries of Christianity* (New York: Herder and Herder, 2006), 266.

10. Parente, *The Angels: In Catholic Teaching and Tradition*, 34.

11. A letter from Saint Clare of Assisi, virgin, to St. Agnes of Prague (Edit. I. Omaechevarria, Escritos de Santa Clara, Madrid 1970, pp. 339–341).

12. Jean Daniélou, *Gospel Message and Hellenistic Culture: A His-*

tory of Early Christian Doctrine Before the Council of Nicea (Philadelphia: The Westminster Press, 1973), 34 ff.

13. Aquinas, *ST*, I, q.108, a.8.

14. H. M. Boudon, *The Glories of the Holy Angels, "An Exhortation to the Love and Honour of the Holy Angels"* (Philadelphia: McGrath).

15. Livio Melina, *Sharing in Christ's Virtues* (Washington, D.C.: The Catholic University of America Press, 2001), 46

16. St. Augustine, *Literal Meaning of Genesis IV,* 22:39 (ACW 41:130); Bonino, *Angels and Demons,* 189.

17. St. Gregory the Great, *Homilies* XXXIV.

18. Aquinas, *ST*, I, q.63, a.7; Ia, q.110, a.1, r.3. St. John Damascene agrees *De Fide. Orth. II,* 4, as does Origen, *Homilies* (14 on the Book of Numbers).

19. Aquinas, *ST*, I, q.62, a.5.

20. St. Leo the Great, *Sermon 1 on the Ascension* 2–4: PL 54, 395–396.

21. Parente, *The Angels: In Catholic Teaching and Tradition,* 64.

22. Scheeben, *The Mysteries of Christianity,* 269.

23. See Aquinas, *ST*, I, q.63, a.1, r.4 and Pope St. John Paul II, Wednesday Catechesis, July 7, 1986.

24. See Balthasar, *Theodrama Theological Dramatic Theory III: Dramatis Personae Man in God,* 487; see Aquinas, *ST*, I, q.63, a.5, r.4; and Bonino, *Angels and Demons,* 3 n. 4.

25. Parente, *The Angels: In Catholic Teaching and Tradition,* 65.

26. St. Cyril of Jerusalem, *Catechetical Lectures* 2.4, *Fathers of the Church: A New Translation* (Washington, D.C.: The Catholic University of America Press, 1947), 61:98; see also Denz. 457.

27. Parente, *The Angels: In Catholic Teaching and Tradition,* 60.

28. Bonino, *Angels and Demons,* 208.

29. Aquinas, *ST*, I, q.63, a.8, sed contra.

30. See also Colossians 2:8 and Galatians 4:3–9.

31. For the connection and reference to angels as stars, see Bonino, *Angels and Demons,* 15 n.11; see also H. M. Féret, OP, *The*

Apocalypse of St. John (Maryland: Newman Press, 1958), 116, for angels commonly referred to as "stars."

32. In Latin, *Lucifer;* see Bonino, *Angels and Demons,* 195, n. 12; for the connection and reference to angels as stars, see Bonino, *Angels and Demons,* 15 n.11; and 205; see also Féret, *The Apocalypse of St. John,* 116, for fallen angels are commonly referred to as "stars"; for this passage referring to Lucifer, see Parente, *The Angels: In Catholic Teaching and Tradition,* 57.

33. St. Augustine, *City of God,* 11.15; Origen, *On First Principles,* I.5.4, trans. G. W. Butterworth (London: SPCK, 1936). Reprint, Glouster, Mass.: Peter Smith, 1073. St. John Cassian, *The Conferences VIII,* VIII, 1–2; 295 – 2 96. See also, Stanzione, *Essential Guide to Angels,* 41 and Parente, *The Angels: In Catholic Teaching and Tradition,* 42, 58.

34. Boudon affirms that the precious stones point to the various perfections of the angels ("Devotion to the Holy Angels," in *The Glories of the Holy Angels,* First Part. Motive the First).

35. Daniélou explains in Daniel, as with the Prince of Tyre in Ezekiel, the references to the King of Persia are not men but angelic powers, see Daniélou, *Origen,* 230; see also Bonino, *Angels and Demons,* 195.

36. St. Augustine clarifies that this does not refer to the beginning wherein Lucifer was created, but from the beginning of sin (*De Civ. Dei* xi, 15; Aquinas, *ST,* I, q.63, a.5, r.1.)

37. Aquinas, *ST,* I, q. 63, a. 7; see I-II, q.80, a.4 see S.T. Bonino, *Angels and Demons,* 51.

38. Scheeben, *The Mysteries of Christianity,* 264.

39. St. Jerome, *Homilies on the Psalms,* Psalm 14, Fathers of the Church, 48:107.

40. Aquinas, *ST,* I, q.63, a.6; see, Saint Augustine, *On the Literal Interpretation of Genesis,* iv, 24.

41. Venerable Bede, *Commentary on Luke* Lib 1, 46–55: CCL 120, 37–39.

42. Pope St. John Paul II, Wednesday Catechesis, July 23, 1986

and August 13, 1986; Parente, *The Angels: In Catholic Teaching and Tradition*, 35, 47; W. Farrell, OP, *The Devil*, 30.

43. See Pope St. John Paul II, *Jesus, Son and Savior: A Catechesis on the Creed (Boston: Pauline, 1996)*, 30; see also Scheeben, *The Mysteries of Christianity*, 270; Bonino, *Angels and Demons*, 205, 218; and Balthasar, *Theodrama IV: The Action*, 197–198.

Chapter Five

1. See Pope St. Paul VI, General Audience, November 15, 1972.

2. See Pope St. John Paul II, Wednesday Audience, August 13, 1986, and W. Farrell, OP, *The Devil*, 9.

3. Jean Daniélou, *Advent* (New York: Sheed and Ward, 1951), 143; Jean Daniélou, *Holy Pagans of the Old Testament* (New York: Longmans, Green and Co LTD, 1957), 37; and Hans Urs von Balthasar, *Theologic III: The Spirit of Truth* (San Francisco: Ignatius Press, 2005), 389.

4. Daniélou, *The Angels and their Mission*, 45.

5. Farrell, *The Devil*, 45.

6. Paul Claudel, *A Poet Before the Cross* (Chicago: Henry Regnery Company), 106.

7. Origen, *Homily on Genesis*, 9, 3 as in Daniélou, *Origen*, 233.

8. See John Cassian, *Conferences* VIII, Chapter X.

9. Balthasar, *Theodrama: Theological Dramatic Theory III: Dramatis Personae Persons in Christ*, 486.

10. Cassian, The Conferences VII, XXXII.5; Ramsey edition, 271; see W. Farrell, OP, *The Devil*, 12.

11. John Cassian, *Conferences* VIII, Chapter X.

12. Hans Urs von Balthasar, *Theodrama: Theological Dramatic Theory IV: The Action* (San Francisco: Ignatius Press, 1994), 160.

13. St. John Chrysostom, *Commentary on Job Patristische Texte und Studien* (New York: de Gruyter, 1964), 35:24; 1.17

14. See Heinrich Schlier, *Principalities and Powers in the New Testament*, (Edinburgh: Nelson, 1961), chapter 1; and Hans Urs von Balthasar, *Theo Drama Theological Dramatic Theory IV: The Action*,

148.

15. Lyonnet, *The Meditation on the Two Standards and its Scriptural Foundation*, 12.

16. Féret, *The Apocalypse of St. John*, 113.

17. St. Teresa of Avila, *Interior Castle* in *The Collected Works of St. Theresa of Avila*, Vol. 2; (Washington, D.C.: ICS Publications, 1980), I:2, 15; 295.

18. Lyonnet, *The Meditation on the Two Standards and its Scriptural Foundation*, 2.

19. Bouyer, *The Spirituality of the New Testament and the Fathers*, 310.

20. Ibid.

21. Walter Farrell, OP, *The Devil*, 12.

22. Bouyer, *The Spirituality of the New Testament & the Fathers*, 310.

23. Herman Hendrickx, *The Parables of Jesus: Studies in the Synoptic Gospels* (San Francisco: Harper and Row, 1983), 54–55.

24. Simon Tugwell, OP, *Ways of Imperfection: An Exploration of Christian Spirituality* (Illinois: Templegate, 1985), 25.

25. Aquinas, *ST*, I, q.111, a.4.

26. Ibid., a.2, 3.

27. Ibid., a.1, 4; I-II, q.9, a.6 and q.80, a.2. See Pope St. John Paul II, Wednesday Catechesis, August 13 and 20, 1986; F. M. Catherine "Demoniacs in the Gospel" as in W. Farrell, OP, *The Devil*, 91.

28. Aquinas, *ST*, I, q.111, a.2, r.2.

29. Ibid., q.57, a.4, sed contra.

30. See Bonino, *Angels and Demons*, 150.

31. St. John Cassian, *The Conferences* VII, XII.1; VII, XIV.1, 2; and VII, XV.4; Ramsey edition, 256–258. See also, Boudon, *The Glories of the Holy Angels*, First Part, Motive Eighth.

32. Stanzione, *Essential Guide to Angels*, 62–63.

33. See Gabriel Bunge, *Dragon's Wine and Angel's Bread: The Teaching of Evagrius Ponticus on Anger and Meekness* (New York: St.

Vladimir's Seminary Press, 2009), 61.

34. See St. Theresa of Avila, *The Interior Castle*, II.1.4, 299.

35. St. John Cassian, *The Conferences*, IX, 36.1, 353.

36. Schlier, *Principalities and Powers in the New Testament*, 36.

37. Lyonnet, *The Meditation on the Two Standards and its Scriptural Foundation*, 8.

38. See Farrell, *The Devil*, 13, 23, 33; and Parente, *The Angels: In Catholic Teaching and Tradition*, 26–28, 62.

39. Dionysius, *The Divine Names*, 4.23.

40. Aquinas, *ST*, I, q.109, a.1; see I, q.112, a.3.

41. Daniélou, *The Lord of History*, 15; see also Heinrich Schlier, *Principalities and Powers in the New Testament* (London: Nelson, 1961), 38.

42. Pope St. John Paul II, Wednesday Catechesis, August 13, 1986.

43. Schlier, *Principalities and Powers in the New Testament*, 17.

44. Simon Tugwell, *The Beatitudes: Soundings in Christian Tradition* (London: Darton, Longerman and Todd, LTD, 1980), 17.

45. See Derek DelGaudio, *Amoralman: A True Story and Other Lies* (New York: Alfred A. Knopf, 2021), 212.

46. Herman Hendrickx, *The Parables of Jesus*, 107.

Chapter Six

1. Lyonnet, *The Meditation on the Two Standards and its Scriptural Foundation*, 9.

2. See Balthasar, *Theodrama: Theological Dramatic Theory IV: The Action*, 21, 77.

3. St. Teresa of Avila, *The Book of Her Life* in *Saint Teresa of Avila, Collected Works: The Book of Her Life, Spiritual Testimonies, Soliloquies* Second Edition, Trans. Kieran Kavanaugh, O.C.D., and Otilio Rodriguez, O.C.D., Vol. 1, (Washington, D.C.: ICS Publications, 1987), chapter 15; 144.

4. Claudel, *A Poet Before the Cross*, 6.

5. See Johann Hari, *Stolen Focus: Why You Can't Pay Attention—And*

How to Think Deeply Again (New York: Crown, 2022).

6. "When you are checking your phone or spending time surfing websites, you are effectively in a different environment. You have gone somewhere else. You are not present in real-world terms." Mary Aken, PhD, *The Cyber Effect* (New York: Random House, 2016), Kindle Edition.

7. See Claudel, *A Poet Before the Cross,* 118.

8. St. Teresa of Ávila, *The Book of Her Life,* 99.

9. St. Teresa of Ávila, *The Interior Castle,* 351, 298, 299, and 315.

10. Ibid., 333.

11. Aquinas, *ST,* I, q.112, a.3, r.3.

12. See St. Francis de Sales, *Introduction to the Devout Life,* chapter 29

13. Aquinas, *ST,* I, q.110, a.4.

14. See Fr. Pat Collins, C.M., *Freedom from Evil Spirits: Released from Fear, Addiction and the Devil* (Dublin: Columba Books, 2019), 156.

15. Aquinas, *ST,* I, q.114, a.4.

16. Origen, *Homily Hier,* lat. I, 4.

17. Serge-Thomas Bonino, OP, *Angels and Demons: A Catholic introduction* (Washington, D.C.: The Catholic University of America Press, 2016), 25.

18. Daniélou, *Origen,* 240.

19. Daniélou, *The Lord of History,* 31.

20. A. Hamman, "Magic." *Encyclopedia of Ancient Christianity Volume II Institutum Patristicum Augustinianum* (Illinois: IVP Academic), 654.

21. Saint Justin Martyr, *1 Apol.* 26, 1-3; 56, 2; *Dial.* 120, 6.

22. See Bonino, *Angels and Demons,* 147 and 287.

23. Cassian notes that the demons cannot on their own even enter the herd of swine in the country of the Gerasenes: "The demons pleaded with him, 'If you drive us out, send us into the herd of swine'" (Mt. 8:31). Cassian tells us: "If they have no power to go into the unclean and mute animals without the permission of God, all the more should we believe that they are unable of their own will to enter into human beings who have been created in the image of God." See also, Farrell, OP, *The Devil,*

68.

24. See Bonin, *Angels and Demons, 80.*

25. Aquinas, *ST*, I, q.114, a.3, arg.3, et ad, 3.

Chapter Seven

1. Bouyer, *The Meaning of the Monastic Life*, 28.

2. See Balthasar, *The Glory of the Lord VII: Theology — The New Covenant*, 45; 70; see Balthasar's reflection on "Community out of loneliness" in *Explorations in Theology IV: Spirit and Institution* (San Francisco: Ignatius Press, 1995), 270–271ff.

3. Hans Urs von Balthasar, *The Glory of the Lord: A Theological Aesthetics VI: The Old Covenant* (San Francisco: Ignatius Press, 1991), 223.

4. See Laurie Gottlieb, *Maybe You Should Talk to Someone* (New York: Houghton, Mifflin, Harcourt, 2019), 233.

5. Louis Bouyer, *The Spirituality of the New Testament & the Fathers* (New York: Descless Company, 1960), 313.

6. Ibid.

Chapter Eight

1. See Bonino, *Angels and Demons*, 5, n.9.

2. See St. Augustine, *On Genesis: Two Books on Genesis Against the Manichees* trans. Roland J. Teske, SJ (Washington, D.C.: The Catholic University of America Press, 1991), 113.

3. St. Ignatius of Antioch, *Letter to the Trallians, Caput, 7*, 1–8; *Funk 1*: 209.

4. St. Teresa of Ávila, *The Book of Her Life as in The Collected Works of St. Teresa of Avila*, 13.18, 131.

5. Parente emphasizes the famous problem that had engaged the attention of Scripture scholars for decades: The angel of the Lord in the Old Testament, who is represented as acting in the name of God himself — and is often received and honored as God would be honored — is truly an angel. Parente notes that the "opinion which holds that the expression 'Angel of the Lord' is not really an Angel, or Saint Michael, but the Word

of God (the Logos) God himself, is now regarded as mere conjecture and a rather obsolete opinion." *The Angels: In Catholic Teaching and Tradition*, 92, 94. Parente draws on W. G. Heidt, *Angelology of the Old Testament*, 96 ff, as echoing the same understanding. See also Graham A. Cole, *Against the Darkness: The Doctrine of Angels, Satan, and Demons* (Illinois: Crossway, 2019), 62, 64; Pope St. John Paul II, Wednesday Catechesis, July 9, 1986.

    6. St. Ambrose, *On the Holy Spirit*, 1, Prologue, 1.

Chapter Nine

    1. Daniélou, *Origen*, 223.

    2. Balthasar, *The Glory of the Lord: A Theological Aesthetics VII: Theology – The New Covenant*, 75.

    3. Tertullian, *On Baptism*, I.

    4. Ibid., III.

    5. Louis Bouyer, *The Spirituality of the New Testament & the Fathers*, 313.

    6. Balthasar, *Theodrama: Theological Dramatic Theory IV: The Action*, 160.

    7. The author is grateful for Dr. Andrew Lichtenwalner for this insight in private correspondence.

Chapter Ten

    1. Boudon, *Devotion to the Holy Angels, First Part*, "The Admirable Perfections of These Blessed Spirits," 3.

    2. St. John Chrysostom, *Homilies on the Gospel of John*, 86.1.

    3. St. Augustine, *Sermo Guelferbytanus*, 3: PLS 2, 545–546.

    4. See Collins, *Freedom from Evil Spirits: Released from Fear, Addiction and the Devil*, 163–164.

    5. Lyonnet, *The Meditation on the Two Standards and its Scriptural Foundation*, 12.

    6. Boudon, *The Glories of the Holy Angels*, First Part, Motive Eighth.

7. St. Teresa of Ávila, *The Interior Castle*, 333; see,Tobit 13:13; see Parente, *The Angels: In Catholic Teaching and Tradition*, 141.

8. Boudon, *The Glories of the Holy Angels*, "The Protection afforded to us by the Angels against the enemies of our Salvation," First Part, Motive Eighth.

9. St. Athanasius, *Paschal Epistle 3* (NPNF 2:4), 1232.

10. Anonymous, *Cloud of Unknowing* (Boulder: Shambhala, 2009), ch. 23, 60.

11. Parente, *The Angels: In Catholic Teaching and Tradition*, 134–135, and Boudon, *The Glories of the Holy Angels*, "Devotion to the Nine Choirs of Angels," Second Part, Practice First.

12. St. Teresa of Ávila, *The Interior Castle*, 320.

13. Adrienne von Speyr, *Mark: Meditation on the Gospel of Mark* (San Francisco: Ignatius Press, 2012), 30.

14. Schlier, *Principalities and Powers in the New Testament*, 45, n. 38.

15. Aquinas, *ST*, I, q.108, a.8, r.2. see St. Augustine, *De cura pro mortuis* xiii, xvi.

16. Luke Dysinger, O.S.B., "Evagrius Ponticus: The Psalter as a Handbook for the Christian Contemplative," *The Harp of Prophecy: Early Christian Interpretation of the Psalms* (Indiana: University of Notre Dame Press, 2015), 103.

17. Pope St. John Paul II, *Rosarium Virginis Mariae*, 4.

18. See Bonino, *Angels and Demons*, 36; see Schlier, *Principalities and Powers in the New Testament*, 51.

19. Daniélou, *The Lord of History*, 15.

20. From an exposition of Psalm 118 by St. Ambrose, Cap. 20:43-45, 48: CSEL 62, 466-368.

21. See Balthasar, *Theodrama V: The Last Act*, 210.

22. From the Rule of Saint Benedict, abbot (*Prologus*, 4-22; cap. 72, 1-12; CSEL 75, 2-5, 162-163).

ABOUT THE AUTHOR

Rev. Msgr. J. Brian Bransfield is a priest of the Archdiocese of Philadelphia. He holds a doctorate in moral theology from the Pontifical John Paul II Institute for Studies on Marriage and Family. He has served on the faculty of Saint Charles Borromeo Seminary, as general secretary of the USCCB, and as a lecturer at The Catholic University of America and adjunct faculty at The Dominican House of Studies in Washington, D.C. He serves as pastor of St. Joseph Parish in Aston, Pennsylvania. He is the author of several books including *The Human Person: According to John Paul II* and *Living the Beatitudes: A Journey to Life in Christ.*